ONE GOD FOR ALL

DIL R. BANU

Copyright @2020 by DIL BANU (Third Edition)

All rights reserved. No part of this book may be reproduced in any form or by any electronic or mechanical means, including information storage and retrieval systems, without permission in writing from the publisher, except by reviewers, who may quote brief passages in a review.

This publication contains the opinions and ideas of its author. It is intended to provide helpful and informative material on the subjects addressed in the publication. The author and publisher specifically disclaim all responsibility for any liability, loss or risk, personal or otherwise, which is incurred as a consequence, directly or indirectly, of the use and application of any of the contents of this book.

WORKBOOK PRESS LLC
187 E Warm Springs Rd,
Suite B285, Las Vegas, NV 89119, USA

Website:	https://workbookpress.com/
Hotline:	1-888-818-4856
Email:	admin@workbookpress.com

Ordering Information:
Quantity sales. Special discounts are available on quantity purchases by corporations, associations, and others. For details, contact the publisher at the address above.

Library of Congress Control Number: 2018936919
ISBN-13:   978-1-953839-39-8 (Paperback Version)
           978-1-953839-40-4 (Digital Version)

REV. DATE: 18.03.2021

Dedication

This book is dedicated for all God-loving and truth-seeking people who believe in God and also hope to return to Him safely following His revealed guidance.

Table of Contents

- i   Pacific Book Review/ One God for all By Rae C Bernard
- iii   Why I needed to write this book
- x   Acknowledgements
- xi   Reference and resources
- 01   Letter 1. The God of Judeo-Christian Faith and The God of Islam
- 12   Letter 2. The Holy Quran Says, God Is One and Only
- 19   Letter 3. Both Parts of the Holy Bible Proclaim: God Is One and Only
- 25   Letter 4. Muhammad Was Sent Reviving and Restoring Abraham's Faith, in Islam
- 37   Letter 5. Jesus' Comforter Was Muhammad, the Prophet of Islam
- 53   Letter 6. True Meaning and Implication of the Name "Christ" and "Word"
- 66   Letter 7. Jesus Was Declared a Prophet of God in both Gospel and Quran
- 73   Letter 8. Jesus as the "Son of God" and as the "Son of Man"
- 80   Letter 9. Trinity Was Invented after Jesus Left, He Never Taught It
- 95   Letter 10. Some Misunderstood and Misinterpreted Statements of Jesus
- 107   Letter 11. Jesus Never Said or Did Anything but by the Command of God
- 117   Letter 12. "Our Only Way to Heaven" as described in Bible and Quran
- 154   Afterword---An Unexpected Disruption
- 157   Bibliography
- 160   Feedback from other distinguished readers
- 164   About Reverend Franklin Graham
- 165   About the Author
- 166   About the Book
- 167   Pacific Book Review about Author's Second Book
- 169   Author's Next Book

Pacific Book Review

ONE GOD FOR ALL

By Rae C. Bernard

There is always a comparison and contrast to both spiritual texts, between the Bible and the Quran, on whose God is better or most powerful. Surprisingly, the debate will forever remain between Judeo-Christians and Muslims, until both sides become more open-minded to the possibility of a One God, no matter what name is preferred for reference. In One God for All, author Dil R. Banu ensures readers that God is one and the same regardless of what another religion, specifically of Islam are calling Him, by providing evidence from both spiritual texts. People are always trying to prove there is a difference between what they believe versus others they encounter and this book demonstrates otherwise. By reading this book, you will gain a level of open mindfulness maybe there is more than what you've been raised or taught to believe. You learn the text in both the Quran and the Bible share unexpected similarities, especially for someone who have never read both books of spiritual texts.

Jesus and Muhammad are the most important individuals in each book because they are the last of God/Allah's messengers for the people on earth. One would be fascinated in learning that both messengers were created to fulfill similar purposes. This grants the ability to step outside of your in-box thinking and consider the proof provided to you, encouraging the overall goal of a One God for everyone. Of course, one would think because there are different books, there would be different views on what is believed and it's not the case with this book. Not once has the author critiqued or opted to project her views onto the readers, setting the reading experience in more of an educational tone.

The author used letters as a method to educate readers, which shows various correspondences with a reverence about specific Holy Scriptures. This enables clarity for those assuming that the beliefs of Muslims are not the same as those of Judeo-Christians. Personally, knowing Jesus was the created son brought down by God to provide a sacrifice for His people, was interesting to learn that Muhammad had a similar role. It is a true eye-opener discovering that prophets and messengers had a particular task to aid the evolving world and its inhabitants. Either beliefs want its people to remain on a righteous path, following the rules/commandments of God/Allah or it is up to individual to uphold their end of the agreement.

I have never had the opportunity to read the Quran in my entire life; I was amazed by the way their text had instances like the Bible. In learning this, I started to come to understand just how strong the Islamic beliefs are and why they seem hardcore to do anything in the name of Allah. I felt that I can take away quite a few scriptures from the Quran that are in agreeance with the Bible and knowing that they too want the same thing for their lives and their people. I am very appreciative of the author for delving into both books and finding Scriptures from each to aid her case that we all believe in One God, and only one alone. The book is a well-written filled with personal research, spending time in gathering the proper evidence to provide clarity to readers. I highly recommend anyone who wants to discover for themselves just how similar both spiritual books can be to consider reading One God for all, as the author saved her readers time and the necessity for having to read both.

In the name of God, Most Compassionate, Most Merciful

Why I needed to write this book

I think, a book like this requires a preface so that my prospective readers know in advance what motivated an old, ordinary, and unknown woman like me to write about such a highly sensitive, speculative and metaphysical subject as God. But before I go into that, I would like to mention first the contents of this book though meant for the Christians, people of other faiths who believe in God and in the eternal life after death, will find this book useful and worth- reading. I also like to request both my Christian and non-Christian friends to consider this book as a kind of religious journal, where I have tried to report what I have observed, studied, learned or felt about the religious faith of the common, simple and devoted Christians while living with them as my neighbors, co-workers, and friends since I settled in America as an immigrant nearly three decades ago. I also added a few things about me and some of my experiences so that my readers may understand clearly why I chose this delicate, sensitive, and controversial subject for my writing.

I am a non-Arab Muslim by birth and practice.

My homeland is Bangladesh-a beautiful country in South-East Asia. I was fifty when I first came to America-the land of my childhood-dream and settled in a city of Maryland. Within the first few days of my arrival, I understood clearly that I came here not only from a different race and religion, I also carried with me a bagful of different customs, culture, language, and lifestyle. But I also had with me the maturity of my age and a set way of life of a practicing Muslim that helped me greatly to cope with those changes while keeping my old ways of life unchanged. Besides that, my degree in Education and a long experience of teaching in one of the prestigious schools of my country, also helped me greatly to have a job of a substitute teacher in the local elementary schools, soon after I came here.

Change of job became a turning point in my life

After a year or so, I gave up teaching and opened a licensed family day care in my rented apartment, where all my neighbors were Christians. I still am grateful to God to help me choose the job of a childcare provider over the job of a teacher. This change of job became a turning point in my life. It finally made me a writer from a childcare provider. At this point, I also like to mention that Comparative Religion was my favorite subject since my teenage. I always had a keen fascination to know about God and His religions that people in different places of the world practices in His name. So, I became a bit excited when I came in close contact with bunches of cute and lovely kids-both white and colored along with their parents or guardians, soon after I started running my daycare. I also had other good reasons that made me feel closer to them.

People of the Book

I had known about Jesus and his followers in details from my mid-twenties, when I first started reading the meaning and interpretation of the Noble Quran-the text of which was revealed to Prophet Muhammad in Arabic, about fourteen hundred years ago. In many places of the Quran, the Jews and the Christians were addressed as the "People of the Book," because they also received their Holy Books the Torah, the Psalms, and the Gospel through Moses, David, and Jesus respectively. But this is the first time in America I met them in person and began to know them closely.

Abraham's place in the Quran

The Quran has addressed Abraham as the leader of many nations and called him often *hanif* meaning the upholder of pure and pristine monotheism. The Quran also tells us the Jews, the Christians, and the Muslims have inherited their faith through Abraham. May be, it is for that long and deep-rooted link or heritage of our faith, I felt myself very much connected with my Christian neighbors and friends, even though I knew there was a heaven-to-earth difference in what we both believe and practice in the name of the same God.

The Christians are nearest in affection to the Muslims

I tried to ignore those differences after I began to live my day to day life with the Christians as my neighbors, friends, and the parents of my Daycare children. I found them so kind, loving, friendly, and helpful that they often reminded me of that particular verse in the Quran, where God has said, *You will find nearest in affection to the believers [Muslims] are those, who say: We are Christians. (5:82)*

As the days rolled by, I began to feel a strong urge inside me to tell them of what the Quran has really said about Jesus, what he taught and what he never taught. But I could not. I felt religion was a very delicate and sensitive subject, and the topic of my discussion also seemed to me more critical. How could I tell them they had been following something in the name of Jesus which he never taught? Then, one day to my utter surprise, the chance of talking about Jesus came to me quite unexpectedly. About a year or so, after I started my Family Daycare, I had a chance to know many Christian Missionaries who began visiting me in my apartment unannounced. They used to come in a group consisting of two to three men, women, young and old both. The sole purpose of their visit was, I soon learned, to make me aware that my salvation was at stake, and what I needed to do to save me from the fire of hell. They also flooded me with books, booklets, magazines, leaflets, or fliers, whenever they came to visit me. As religion was my favorite subject, I used to read them all most willingly from cover to cover. And I felt really amazed to know the bottom line of all those printed materials was the same as they had been telling me repeatedly since I met them first. It was "No Jesus, No Heaven."

Most of them remained unaware of the mainstream Islam

So, naturally, I availed this chance and tried to tell them what the Quran said about Jesus and why he was sent for. At first, I felt myself astonished to know that most of my missionary friends remained unaware of the mainstream Islam and therefore, the name of Muhammad as the last Prophet of God and the name of the Quran, as His last and the final guidebook remained unknown to them. Or, if they knew anything at all, it was either wrong or misleading. As for example, many of them mistook the

Arab Prophet Muhammad of the seventh century for Elijah Muhammad, a black American and the founder of Nation of Islam in Chicago only a few decades ago. I tried to correct those mistakes as humbly as possible. I found them quite pleased, when I described to them what the Quran says in adoration of Mary, and her son Jesus including his miraculous birth, the miracles he performed, his ascent to heaven alive, his second coming, and the special status or rank that he and his mother received from God. But they began to visit me less frequently after I started telling them that Jesus were not a deity or an inseparable part of God as they believed. Rather, he was a noble and a righteous human being whom God chose as His messenger for the guidance of his own people-the misguided Jews.

I took the study of the Bible seriously

Soon I understood my mistake. I was telling them about Jesus as I learned from the Quran-the Book we believe ourselves as the last and the final guidebook of God for all of mankind. But they claim, it is only the Bible that contains true guidance of God. Some of my missionary friends also told me very politely that they would not accept anything to be true, if they find it inconsistent or contradictory to the statements of their Holy Bible. So I thought, they might have listened to me carefully and seriously if I could tell them about Jesus's role and mission from the Gospel, the Book they believe themselves as the true account of Jesus' own words and deeds. As soon as I understood it, I took the study of the Bible very seriously.

One of my missionary friends gave me a copy of Bible in the King James Version which I used to read in a sporadic manner. In this way, I completed most of the chapters in the Gospel. But to establish Jesus' status as a Messenger of God, I needed to read both parts of the Bible minutely. With this intention in mind, I started reading the Bible thoroughly beginning from Genesis, the first book of Moses.

Both Parts of the Bible proclaim: God is One and only

Frankly speaking, my faith in the Quran became stronger and more intensified when I found both parts of the Holy Bible also proclaim God is One and Only, and no one is worthy of worship besides Him. It was then,

I felt for the first time to share this common heritage of our faith with the audience of the Western world through my writing and publishing it in a book. I not only felt, I began to write about it without wasting my time. The question of looking for a publisher arose after I finished my writing within a year or so. But all my spirit or excitement fused off instantly, when I contacted a well-known Muslim Publisher who appreciated my intention and effort but regretted to publish because the subject-matter of my writing seemed to him quite controversial. Without making any further attempt, I saved my hand-written manuscript in a drawer of my file-cabinet. Then along with my daily chores, I engaged myself in watching the end-game of the 2000 Presidential campaign in between George W. Bush and Al Gore, in either CNN or MSNBC-two of my favorite channels.

Prayer followed by an anti-Islamic propaganda

After Mr. Bush won the election, I was watching the live telecast of his presidential inauguration on January 20, 2001. In that ceremony, Reverend Franklin Graham, the well-reputed evangelist, and a well-known missionary of America, offered a prayer that I found quite interesting. I felt myself elated when I heard him to say his prayer just like a Muslim. He said, "Now, O Lord, we dedicate this presidential inaugural ceremony to You. May this be the beginning of a new dawn for America as we humble ourselves before You and acknowledge You alone as our Lord, our Savior, and our Redeemer." And then, of course, he finished his prayer like a devoted Christian. He said, "We pray this in the name of the Father, and of the Son-the Lord Jesus Christ, and of the Holy Spirit. Amen."

While listening to the last part of his prayer, I asked myself wondering, how could a great evangelist like Rev. Graham, make his prayer in the name of the three right after he acknowledged God alone as being his only Lord, Savior, and Redeemer?

Muslims worship a 'different god' and practice a very evil and wicked religion

But I did not know then, more surprises were waiting for me. In the same occasion, Rev. Graham chose to volunteer some unsolicited comment about the God of the Muslims and their religion, Islam. He said "The god of Islam is not the same God of the Christians or the Judeo-Christian faith. It is a different god, and I believe Islam is a very evil and a very wicked religion." He said it openly before thousands of his invited guests and million others both Christians and non-Christians watching the ceremony like me before their TV set:

His comment worked as a jump-start for me

The evangelist made this comment prior to 9/11. So I had no clue what he really intended to mean by this "different god" of the Muslims or what made him blurt out with this kind of slanderous comment against their religion Islam which is now adhered nearly by one fourth population of the world? Whatever his intention was, it worked as a jump start for me. I found his comment totally misleading and malicious for the common and ordinary Christians who hardly knew anything about Islam or its adherents called Muslim. I instantly thought of my manuscript "One God For All" where I tried to present the One Eternal God for all of mankind and the basic truth of His guidance as it has been described in both parts of the Holy Bible and also in His last guidebook-the Quran. I only needed to re-write it with a different approach. I decided to write to the evangelist some open letters in reply to the first part of his comment where he said, 'the god of Islam is different from the God of the Christians or the Judeo-Christian faith.'

I thanked God most gratefully to make me wait so long, until the time and situation was right or ready for me. I also thanked the evangelist in silence to make my work so easy and convenient for me. There was something more which made the load of my work exceptionally light and easy for me. It was a dazzling piece of Toshiba-a brand-new laptop that I received as a birthday gift from my newly married son and his beloved wife just before I began to re-write my manuscript in my worst possible handwriting. My precious daughter-in law also showed me first how to use the keyboard and other related things which made me free forever from the tedious and time-killing job of writing by hand.

After I finished writing, my beloved daughter-a computer-specialist, took care of the rest related to the review, editing and publication of my book. Despite of all those help and co-operation, I had to keep my manuscript on a file of my laptop for more than a decade. Some catastrophic incident took place quite unexpectedly, and it made me forget completely that I ever wrote a book and wanted to publish it for my Christian friends in the Western world. I have narrated all about it in a separate chapter at the end of this book.

It is the third edition of my book since I published it first through Author House Publication in 2014. If God permits, I intend to write my next book under the title, "Islam-the terminator of all evils" in reply to the evangelist's second part of the comment where he said, "I believe, Islam is a very evil and a very wicked religion."

Last of all, I would humbly ask my readers, especially my Christian friends to keep in mind that I wrote this book not to hurt anybody's faith or feeling. I wrote it for the people of all faiths so that they may try to know each other's faith and practices directly from the scriptures of God, and not from their religious gurus or guides. I also want them to know that I am always ready to correct my mistake, if they find me misquote or misinterpret anything from the Holy Bible, the Quran or from any other book that I used for information or reference.

May God kindly help us all to identify His true Path and to follow it correctly until the last moment of our life!

Dil R. Banu
Maryland, USA
November 7, 2020

Acknowledgement

I took this project of writing in the name of God and absolutely for the sake of His pleasure. It is God Almighty Who helped me complete my job under His constant care, mercy, and guidance. So, I thank my Lord most humbly and gratefully to choose me for this job though I do not deserve it anyway.

I also like to remember God in endless gratitude to bless me with a loving, caring and a responsible daughter and a son along with their supportive families. It is for their continuous help and co-operation I was able to concentrate myself on my study and writing. May God kindly protect them all under His special love, mercy, and guidance.

I also wish the same for all my friends and relatives, especially my lion-hearted uncle Quazi Muhammad Hafiz, and Amanullah-my most polite and humble cousin brother along with their loving and caring families for their unconditional support, when I first came to America and needed it most.

I like to offer my heartfelt thanks and gratitude to all my learned reviewers who, despite of their busy schedule, have spent their valuable time in reading my manuscript and above all, for writing their kind notes of appreciation to enhance the value and worth of my book. The review done by Rae C. Barnard in the Pacific Book Review has certainly added the weight and importance of my book.

Similarly, I also like to thank Reverend Franklin Graham and all my missionary friends sincerely and gratefully for their indirect but indispensable role to help me present my book in the printed form out of the unread file of my laptop. May our Almighty and Merciful God be pleased with them and help them all to strive for His Cause.

Last but not the least, I like to convey my special thanks to the Author House Publication to become the first Publisher of my book when others found it controversial.

Salutation on Prophet Muhammad and other Prophets of God

I believe, my Muslim friends will not forget to invoke God to bestow His peace and blessing upon Prophet Muhammad and all His Prophets whenever they come across with their blessed names.

Reference and Resources

The primary sources of my knowledge, information, and reference are Holy Scriptures-the Bible and the Quran. For the Bible, I consulted the King James Version (KJV), the New International Version (NIV) and the Revised Standard Version (RSV), but I quoted mostly from the first two Versions.

For the Quran, I consulted the meaning and interpretation of the renowned scholars like Ibn Kathir, Mufty Muhammad Shafi, A. Yusuf Ali, Muhammad M. Pickthal, and Muhammad Farooq-i-Azam Malik. But I quoted the meaning of the verses mostly from the last three of them. In this connection, I also like to admit honestly that sometimes I copied their translation as it is, and sometimes I copied them combining all, but always keeping their meaning intact. I did so only to make it plain, simple, and easy for the common and ordinary people of the Western world.

Other Sources

In addition to that, Merriam-Webster's Encyclopedia of World Religions, The Concise Encyclopedia of Islam by Cyril Glasse, the complete works of Ahmed Deedat, and many other valuable books written by the most learned, open-minded and well-reputed scholars of both Eastern and the Western World also helped me greatly to explore, inquire and understand the essence and attributes of God, the role of His messengers and the eternal truth of His message that He revealed through them for the guidance of their people. I have also added a bibliography that I used for study, information, or reference at the end of this book.

Summary of Contents

Letter 1. The God of Judeo-Christian Faith vs. The God of Islam

- The Muslims worship the same One God of Jesus, Moses, and Abraham
- The God of the Judeo-Christian Faith
- The God of Islam
- Why do the Muslims call God Allah?
- Allah and God are synonymous
- The name Allah was known in the Pre-Islamic Arab
- The name Allah existed in the Vedic scripture
- YAWH, Eloah and Elohim were also synonymous to Allah
- YAWH became Jehovah in course of time
- Elohim, the plural form of Eloah also refers to One God
- Jesus invoked God as Eli or Eloi in his last moment on the Cross
- The name Alah was found more appropriate than Elah
- On Alleluia-Points to ponder
- The name Allah is unique and immutable
- The key to man's salvation remains hidden in the name Allah

Letter 2. The Quran Says: "God Is One and Only"

- God is One and without any partner
- God is Omnipotent, and Omniscient
- God is the Creator of the entire heavens and earth
- God is the Planner and the Controller of everything in the universe
- God is the Provider and the Sustainer of all living beings
- God's favors to mankind are beyond any measure
- God is Most Kind, Compassionate and Forgiving
- No one is worthy of worship besides God

Letter 3. Both Parts of the Bible Proclaim, "God Is One and Only"

- Man knew God as their only Lord from the beginning of his existence
- The Everlasting covenant of God made with Abraham and his seeds
- Moses was sent to proclaim the worship of One God and to establish His command
- David surrendered himself completely to the will and command of God
- Solomon also followed the footsteps of his noble father David
- God as described in other Books of the Old Testament
- Men were asked to be prudent in choosing the path of God
- God as described in the Gospel of Jesus
- Jesus says God alone is All-perfect
- Jesus' clear view in keeping the commands of God

Letter 4. Muhammad Was Sent Last, Reviving and Restoring Abraham's Faith, in Islam

- God has chosen the name "Islam" for His religion and "Muslim" for its adherents
- God's guidance began with Adam and Eve before they were sent down to earth
- Noah and other Prophets of God as described in the Quran
- Abraham-a great advocate and upholder of pure and pristine monotheism
- Abraham's descendants also followed the legacy of his faith
- Joseph-great-grandson of Abraham, advised his people to worship none but One God
- Moses was sent to proclaim the worship of One True God among his people
- David submitted himself completely for the Cause of God
- Solomon showed his complete allegiance to the will and the command of God

- Jesus-the noble son of Mary was sent following the footsteps of all his predecessors
- Muhammad arrived last proclaiming the worship of none but One God
- The messengers of God were many, but His message was one
- Causes of man's deviation from the Path of God
- Muhammad was sent last reviving, rectifying, and restoring Abraham's faith in Islam
- Muhammad arrived as the last Reminder and the Warner for all of mankind
- It is not the Muslims it is in fact the Christians Who worship "a different god"

Letter 5. Jesus' Comforter Is Muhammad, the Last Prophet of God

- Jesus' Comforter is not the Holy Ghost, but Muhammad-the last Prophet of God
- The Holy Ghost vs. The Holy Spirit
- The term "Spirit" has been used for both true and false prophet
- "He (Comforter) shall teach you all things and bring all things to your memory (John 14:26)
- Jesus' predictions about his Comforter in John 14, 15, and 16 matches only with Muhammad who came after him
- "The Spirit of Truth," in John 16:13, describes Muhammad accurately
- "He (Comforter) will guide you into all truth." (John 16:13)
- "He shall not speak of himself, but whatsoever he shall hear that he shall speak." (John 16:13)
- "And he will show you things to come." (John 16:13)
- "He [The Spirit of truth] shall glorify me" matches only with Prophet Muhammad
- Jesus' Comforter will come after he leaves refers to none but the

- last Prophet Muhammad
- Jesus' "another Comforter" describes Muhammad-the Prophet of Islam accurately
- "He (Comforter) may abide with you forever," in John 14:16 matches only with Prophet Muhammad
- Jesus meant the Muslims to be his true followers
- Muhammad will abide with his followers as their role model
- Muhammad is remembered aloud ten times a day in most parts of the world
- A moment does not pass when his name is remembered aloud or in silence
- Muhammad will live forever in the writing of the non-Muslim Scholars
- Greek word Periclytos correspond directly to the meaning of both Muhammad and Ahmad
- Paracletos is a corrupt reading for Periclytos
- "The desire of all nations" refers to none but Muhammad-the Prophet of Islam
- Jesus' Testifier is Muhammad-the last and the final Prophet of God

Letter 6. True Meaning and Implication of the Name "Christ" and "Word"

- Both "Christ" and "Messiah" are synonymous
- The oppressed people used to believe God would send His Messiah for their relief
- Other Prophets also had God-given names or titles
- Jesus is known to the Muslims by three significant names
- God chose those special names or titles for Jesus and others for a reason
- An unexpected visitor arrived in the middle of my writing
- In the beginning was the Word, and the Word was with God and

- the Word was God
- Jesus was also mentioned in the Quran as the "Word of God"
- The Bible says: "Let there be," while the Quran says: "Be"
- Interpretation of the "Word" as found in the Modern Versions of the Bible
- On Jesus' Incarnation: A report from Grolier's Encyclopedia
- Transgression was made in the Book of God to validate Jesus' Incarnation

Letter7. Jesus Was Declared a Prophet of God in both Gospel and in the Quran

- The Gospel says clearly Jesus was sent as a Prophet of God
- Jesus made his role and mission clear to his people
- The Quran also testifies Jesus was a chosen Messenger of God from the House of Israel
- Jesus testified himself as a Prophet of God from his cradle
- All the messengers of God were His self-surrendered slaves or servants
- Jesus did everything by the command of God and for the sake of His pleasure
- Opinion of the Anglican Bishops about Jesus: Points to ponder

Letter8. Jesus as the "Son of God" and as the "Son of Man"

- Why did Jesus call God his Father and himself His Son?
- The status of God is the highest of all and no one can attain it by any means
- "Son of God" refers to a righteous person
- "Son of man" refers to a human being
- "Son of God" has been eliminated from Mark 1:1 and Acts 8:37
- "Begotten" has been removed from John 3:16

- The Quran describes God's wrath upon them who ascribe son to Him
- The Quran has addressed Jesus as the "Son of Mary"

Letter 9. Trinity Was Invented after Jesus Left, He Never Taught It

- For there are three that bear record in heaven (1 John 5:7)
- Three of them are made of the same substance
- Trinity to be understood in three states of water
- Jesus had power over entire heavens and earth
- Jesus asked his disciples to baptize all nations in the name of the Three
- The status of the Father, the Son and the Holy Ghost is not the same
- The statement of 1John 5:7 has been discarded to be unauthentic
- The Trinity was produced by the Council of Nicaea in 325 CE
- Christian truth is different from Christian religion
- The Trinity was rejected by the Unitarian Christian
- Jesus' followers chose to remain oblivious to his warning about the manmade doctrines
- The Quran has denounced the Trinity as a clear blaspheme against the oneness of God

Letter 10. Some Misunderstood and Misinterpreted Statements of Jesus

- Clear and conclusive statements made by Jesus
- Some metaphoric and misunderstood statements of Jesus
- "I and my Father are one." (John 10:30)
- "The Father in me, and I am in him." (John 10:38)
- True meaning and significance of Jesus' statements in John 10:30 &38
- Exact number of God: One, Two, Three or Unlimited
- "I am the way, the truth and the life." (John 14:6)
- "He that hath seen me, hath seen the Father." (John 14:9)

- "Take heart son, your sins are forgiven thee." (Matthew 9:2)
- "Before Abraham was, I am." (John 8:58)
- Test of Faith: Points to ponder

Letter11. Jesus Never Said or Did Anything but by the Command of God

- God is greater than all and I (10:29; 14:28)
- God sent Jesus for the guidance of his own people
- Jesus never said or did anything but by the command of God
- Jesus does not forgive, his Father in the heaven does
- Jesus had no place to lay his head
- Jesus needed strength from heaven
- Jesus was not aware of the Last Hour
- Jesus prayed to God more when he was in anguish
- Jesus taught his disciples how to pray to God
- Jesus became vulnerable as he came closer to death
- Jesus felt himself deserted of God's mercy at the last moment
- Jesus' own statements tell us clearly he could no way be equal to God or his Father in heaven
- Jesus' miraculous birth in support of his being equal to God
- Jesus' miraculous acts in support of his being equal to God
- Jesus was worshiped as God by his people
- Jesus was not a deity but a man of flesh and blood
- God has His own unique way to establish the truth over the lies
- "Have faith in God." Jesus answered. (Mark 11:22)
- Jesus left for His followers some precautionary notes as a reminder to them

Letter 12. Our "Only Way to Heaven" as Described in the Bible and the Quran

- Writing on Jesus without his atonement is like the description of the Sun without its light
- Jesus' true status cannot be measured without his Atonement
- Man is born with the stain of Adam's sin
- For all have sinned and fall short before the glory of God
- If sin is breaking the Law of God, how a new-born child becomes a sinner?
- The Old Testament tells us man is responsible for what he does
- The Quran also tells us man is accountable for his own deeds
- The Old Testament tells us repentance is required for the remission of sin
- The Quran also tells us repentance is required for the remission of sin
- The Quran tells us Adam and Eve repented for their being disobedient to God.
- God's guidance for mankind began with Adam and Eve before they were sent to earth
- 'Our only way to heaven' has also remained the same in the teaching of Jesus
- Jesus says Heaven is meant for the children
- God says or acts many ways the mystery of which is beyond our comprehension
- Jesus came to give his life a ransom for many
- Jesus refused to cure a sick girl for her non-Jewish affiliation
- Jesus was sent to call the sinners for repentance
- Jesus was put on the Cross by the Jewish High Priest on a false charge of sedition
- Jesus endured all their taunts and torments to show his love for all human beings

- The Gospel tells us Jesus had no intention to die on the Cross
- Jesus did not want to die for a wrong cause
- Circumstantial evidence to prove Jesus did not die on the Cross
- Resurrection and rising from the dead are not the same
- Jesus' prophecy referring to Jonah nullifies the validity of his atonement and Resurrection both
- Jesus' followers chose to play the role of "Doubting Thomas"

Letter 1

The God of the Judeo-Christian Faith vs. the God of Islam

> *And argue not with the people of the Books (Jews and Christians) except in a better way unless it is with those of them who inflict wrong, and say (to them): "We believe in that which has been revealed to us and in that which has been revealed to you; our God and your God is the Same One God, and to Him we submit as Muslims.*
>
> —*Holy Quran 29:46*

Much Respected Reverend Franklin Graham:

I hope you will excuse me, if I dispute your comment that "the god of Islam is not the same God of the Christians or the Judeo-Christian faith. It is a different god." But before I go into that, I would like to draw your attention to one basic criteria to argue or to determine the truth of a disputed, doubtful, or a controversial issue.

As a man of great learning, wisdom, and insight, you must agree that truth itself is self-evident. It does not require any evidence to prove the truth to be true. If we never learned about the rotation of the earth on its axis, it would remain true until the end of the creation. But the scientists needed to provide sufficient proofs, evidence, and reasonable explanation to establish it as true or to make it acceptable to others.

For some reason, however, you have overlooked this fact and did not give any evidence or explanation of what makes you come up with this kind of comment about the God of the Muslims, which is not only far from true, it also seems to be misleading and malicious.

In your speech at President Bush's first inauguration, of which I have a printed transcript, you wrote "the god of Islam"—using a lowercase "g"—but "the God of the Christians or the Judeo-Christian faith" with a capital G. By this tricky change in the letter G, you made your intention quite clear. Along with it, you also commented that Islam was a "very evil and a very wicked religion," and that made your mission complete. The common Christians who believe everything that their evangelists utter to them, might assume the Muslims worship some god or goddess like the pagans of the ancient world, and practice some barbaric religion called Islam.

Muslims worship the same One God of Jesus, Moses, and Abraham

Reverend, with this preconceived idea or impression about the God of Islam, I don't expect you or any of your people to go through my arguments to see of what kind of God the Muslims really worship, or where exactly their God differs from the God of the Jews and the Christians. Despite of that, I would like to hope that some of your people might read and reflect upon my argument where I will try to explain the Muslims or the followers of Muhammad do not worship any "different god" from the God of the Judeo-Christian Faith. Rather, they always worshiped and still worship the same One God of Jesus, Moses, and Abraham since Muhammad arrived reviving their pure monotheistic faith in Islam. I shall of course, try to establish my claim in the light of both parts of the Bible, the Quran, and other reliable sources. I think, my prospective readers especially my Christian friends will understand my point much better, if I first explain to them what we really mean by the God of the Judeo-Christian faith and the God of Islam.

The God of the Judeo-Christian Faith

The very name indicates that the God of the Judeo-Christian faith refers absolutely to the same One God worshipped by Moses and Jesus and their true followers-the Jews, and the Christians, respectively.

Let me quote a verse separately from both parts of the Bible in support of that.

Moses said pleading to his people: *Hear O Israel: The Lord, our God, is one LORD: Love the LORD your God with all your heart and with all your soul and with all your strength. (Duet 6:4-5)*

In reply to all the lucrative offers of the Satan (Matthew 4:8-9), Jesus said to him in disgust, *Away from me, Satan! For it is written: 'Worship the Lord your God and serve him only. (Matthew 4:10)*

The God of Islam

Similarly, the God of Islam refers to the same One God worshiped by Muhammad-the Prophet of Islam, and his followers-the Muslims. According to the description of the Quran, the God of the Judeo-Christian faith and the God of Islam is one and the same. The eternal truth in the guidance of God, which He sent through all His messengers beginning from Adam to His last Prophet Muhammad, was Tawhid (in Arabic)-the meaning of which is pure and pristine monotheism, where God is claimed to be One and Only, and none has the right to be worshiped except Him. As Tawhid is the essence or the fundamental truth in Islam, it is also called Islamic Monotheism. Out of countless verses in the Quran, I have quoted below only two of them.

(3:2–3) Allah, there is no god but Him; the Living, the Eternal. He has revealed to you this Book [the Quran] with the Truth, confirming the scripture which preceded it, as He revealed the Torah and the Gospel before this.

(2:21–22) O mankind! Worship your Lord Who created you and created those who came before you, that you may become righteous. It is He Who, has made the earth your couch, and the sky your canopy, and sent down rain from the heavens; and brought forth therewith fruits for your sustenance; Therefore, do not set up rivals unto God when you know the truth [that He alone has the right to be worshipped].

Why do the Muslims call God Allah?

As God is the cornerstone of our discussion, I would like to explain first why the Muslims all over the world call or invoke God by the name Allah. I need to do it for some obvious reason. While talking to my missionary friends over the past few years, I had a chance to know the common Christians in America have lots of misconceptions about the name Allah. But I felt astonished to know that many well-reputed and highly ranked people in America also belonged to them, at least in this specific field of knowledge.

It is interesting to note that after the fateful day of September 11, 2001, Lieutenant General William G. Boykin said once clearly and confidently that his God meaning the God of the Christians were real and bigger than Allah meaning the God of the Muslims. But like you Reverend, he also did not bother to explain how he found Allah or the God of the Muslims, being fake or smaller than the God of the Christians.

Even a responsible US senator said once, while referring to the fatal incident of 9/11, the God of the Christians sacrificed His own Son to show His love for them and to take them to heaven, but Allah-the God of the Muslims wanted them to sacrifice their lives to show their love for Him and to go to heaven.

It is for the people like them, I need to explain first why the Muslims call or invoke the Object of their worship by the name Allah.

Allah and God are synonymous

People of the Western world may feel surprised to know that Allah and God are synonymous. Allah is the proper name of the same One God in Arabic. So naturally, this name is not confined to the Muslims alone. All Arabic-speaking people, including the Jews and the Christians of the Arab world also call Him Allah instead of God or by any other name of God. The non-Arab Muslims like me and others all over the world, also call Him Allah, because this name has frequently been used in the text of the Holy Quran, which Prophet Muhammad received from God in his native language Arabic about fourteen hundred years ago. In other words, by the name Allah we mean the same One God of the entire heavens and earth Who created mankind with a definite purpose, made them dwell on earth for an indefinite period to fulfill that purpose, and finally wanted them back to heaven-their eternal abode.

The name Allah was known in the Pre-Islamic Arab

People of the Pre-Islamic Arab, who gradually indulged themselves in idol-worship by forgetting the pure monotheistic faith of Abraham, are also known to invoke their Supreme Deity by the name Allah. Not only that, in case of any emergency, importance, or religious obligation, they used to take their oath or to make their sacrifices in the name of Allah. Thus, the name of Allah was known to the Arabs and was used by them long before the Quran was revealed to Prophet Muhammad. As for example, the name of Muhammad's own father was Abd Allah, meaning the slave or the servant of Allah. Besides that, Kabah-the holy Sanctuary in Makkah was also known to them as Baitullah meaning the House of

Allah since the time of Abraham. But when the Arabs got derailed from the monotheistic faith of Abraham and indulged themselves in the pagan practice of polytheism, they made Allah remote or passive and began to ask His favor through His associates or other deities, whom they worshiped by different names.

The name Allah existed in the Vedic Scriptures

The name Allah existed even in the Veda-the oldest known Scripture of God in ancient India during the period of 1500-1200 BCE. The Veda was written in Sanskrit where the name of Allah appeared as "Ollo". In the mantras or the verses of 9:76:30 and 3:30:10 in Rigveda, the name of Allah has been described being one, omnipresent and omniscient. In fact, the essence of Vedic religion now called "Hindu Dharma" is "Ekam Brahm, devitity naste neh na naste kinchen" in Sanskrit meaning God is only One, there is no second deity, never was, never will be. I have quoted below only two in support of that.

(Rigveda 2:1:3) *The Supreme Being manifests the manifest. He fulfills the desires of the good-natured. He is the Lord. He is omnipresent. He is worthy of all praises. He is the Object of all respect. He is Rich. He is the greatest. He is the Creator of everything, and He has the knowledge of everything.*

(Atharvaveda10:9:29) *That Allah is One Who enters the hearts of men and knows their secrets*

YAWH, Eloah, and Elohim were also synonymous to Allah

In the Hebrew Scriptures of Torah (The Old Testament of the Bible), God never introduced Himself as God. All His prophets were known to receive His message in their own native languages. Since none of them was English-speaking, it is more than obvious they were not familiar with the name of their Lord as God.

It is also interesting to note the Jews considered the name of God was too holy to utter. So, they refrained themselves totally from uttering or articulating the name of God in private or in public. Even their chief rabbis (the spiritual leaders of the Jewish congregation) did not allow His ineffable name to be heard any way or anywhere. As a result of that, they eventually forgot how the name of YaHuwa, Eloah or Elohim were pronounced.

The Hebrew Bible used three names for God. YAWH, Eloah, and Elohim. They have been translated in English as Lord God. In a broader and a deeper sense, all of them carry one universal truth about God's being one, eternal and no one was worthy of worship besides Him.

YAWH became Jehovah in course of time

Both Hebrew and Arabic which the Jews and the Arabs inherited from a common linguistic source, tradition, and culture, go long back to their religious and spiritual leader Abraham. Both the languages therefore, shared some common characteristics.

Originally, both Hebrew and Arabic were written without any vowel sign, which made no problem for the native people. They could read it at ease, even without any vowel sign. Later, they started using vowels for the outsiders who had different native languages. Accordingly, when YAWH was spelled in writing with the use of vowels, it became Yawuha. So Yawuah, Yahuwa or Yahu all referred to God in Hebrew.

"Ya" is a vocative and an exclamatory particle in both Hebrew and Arabic meaning "Oh!" Similarly, Huwa, or Hu, means "He" in both Hebrew and Arabic. So, by Yahuwa or Yahu we mean 'Oh, He!' which the Jews used for God without uttering His name. But when a popular trend developed with the European translators to replace the Y for J, the name YeHoWaH was turned or changed into Jehovah.

As for example, Yael, Yehuda, Yusuf, Yunus, and Yesus became Joel, Judah, Joseph, Jonah, and Jesus respectively, after being translated into English.

It was between the sixth and tenth centuries YAWH-the unpronounced name of God of the Hebrew Bible, became Jehovah- a Judeo-Christian name for God in course of time.

Centuries later, in 1931, Joseph Franklin Rutherford, popularly known as Judge Rutherford, founded a new cult upon this very name and called it Jehovah's Witnesses, to reaffirm Jehovah as the true God and to identify them as God's especially accredited followers who witnessed in this name.

Elohim, the plural form of Eloah also refers to One God

Though Elohim is the plural form of Eloah, it was also used to mean the same one God in Hebrew. At this point, it is also important to note that there are two types of plural in the Hebrew and Arabic languages. One indicates number, and the other shows honor or respect, as it is done in case of any royal proclamation. The king or the president of a country usually mentions "We," to include the members of his cabinet or council in appreciation to their specific jobs they were assigned to help him to run the government. But in case of taking any oath or delivering any special message for the people of his country, he mentions him as "I".

Similarly, God Who is most loving, kind, just and generous used "We" in His last and final guidebook-the Quran to include with Him His Angel Gabriel and all His prophets beginning from Adam-the first vice-gerent on earth to the last Prophet Muhammad, in appreciation to their difficult and dedicated job they were assigned to carry out for the guidance of their people. So, none of my readers should be confused with those verses of the Quran, where God used "We" instead of "I" while delivering His message to Muhammad through Gabriel. I needed to explain it, because some scholars of the Western world are not familiar with this characteristic of the Arabic language and because of that they often get confused and mistake "We" for the Trinity (Father, Son, and Holy Spirit). But nowhere in the Quran, the name of God is mentioned in the plural form.

For example, in the verse 105 of chapter 4, God declares through Muhammad:

We have revealed to you the Book with the Truth so that you may judge between people in accordance with the Right Way which Allah has shown to you, so be not advocate for those who betray trust.

The following chart will explain how the name of One God has been used in both Hebrew and Arabic language.

HEBREW	ARABIC	ENGLISH
Elah	Ilah	God
Ikhud	Ahud	One
YaHuwa	YaHuwa	Oh He
Huwa El Elah	Huwallah	He is God

Jesus invoked God as Eli or Eloi in his last moment on the Cross

Reverend, you may feel amazed to know that all the prophets of God including Jesus, were familiar with the name Allah. I mean they used to invoke God in their own languages, which sounds closer to Allah than God or any other translated name of God. As I mentioned before that none of the prophets was English-speaking, so we do not expect them to call or to invoke their Object of worship by the name God.

In the Gospel that Jesus received from God in his native language Aramaic, we heard him to invoke God desperately as Eli or Eloi in his last moment on the Cross. (Matthew 27:46); (Mark 15:34) Interestingly, this part of Jesus' expression in his native tongue has always been preserved in all the Gospels translated in different languages of the world. At this point, I also like to remind you that any expert linguist in Hebrew, Aramaic, or Arabic, will find the name Eli, Eloi, Elohim, Al, El, Alloah, Elah, Alah, or Allah have been originated from the same root, and all of them also refer to the one, eternal, and self-existing Divine Being Whom the Muslims call Allah in Arabic, while the English-speaking people of the Western world call Him God.

The name Alah was found more appropriate than Elah

A truth-seeking reader may feel amazed to know that in the Hebrew Bible, the name *Allah* appears in almost all the verses of the first book of Genesis as *Elah* or *Alah*. The Scofield Reference Bible in English, edited by Rev. C. I. Scofield, DD (doctor of divinity), along with a team of eight consulting editors, all DDs, found the name *Alah* to be more appropriate while translating the Hebrew name *Elah* from the Book of Genesis. But the name *Alah* has now been wiped out mysteriously from the recent publication of the New Scofield Reference Bible.

On Alleluia—Points to Ponder

There is hardly any Christian who is not familiar with the name *alleluia*. We find this name in the book of Revelation (19:1)-the last book of the New Testament. This verse describes a vision of John-a disciple of Jesus.

He heard the angels in heaven say *alleluia* in praise of God. The Christians, in general, also exclaim the name *alleluia* when they go into some sorts of ecstasy or uplift in spirit. They do it however, without knowing the true meaning or the implication of what they utter to express the devotion of their hearts. They may feel surprised to know that by the exclamation of *alleluia*, they express their feeling of joy or gratitude to God by calling Him, *"Oh Eli, Alle, Elah, Alah or Allah."*

As previously mentioned, Ya is used as a vocative or an exclamatory particle, meaning "Oh!" in the language of both Hebrew and Arabic. Accordingly, any Arab or Jew would pronounce alleluia as *Ya-Alle-Lu*, meaning, *"Oh Eli, Alle, Elah, Alah or Allah"* as I mentioned above.

Don't you think Reverend, this explanation matches with "Allah" much better than God or any other familiar or translated name of God?

The name Allah is unique and immutable

The name "Allah" is original, unique, and immutable in many ways.

First, Allah has no corresponding word in English or in any other known language of the world.

Second, no new or corresponding word can be made from Allah, as it is done with the name God. For example: goddess, godfather, godson, and godly.

Third, the name Allah has neither any plural, masculine nor feminine form, as we have with God.

Fourth, the name **Allah** has remained unchanged and immutable since God has revealed this name for Him to be invoked and worshiped by men. The Muslim however, believes the name Allah and His Words will remain intact until the end of the world as it is now, fulfilling His promise that He made in the Quran about fourteen hundred years ago through His last Prophet Muhammad.

The key to man' salvation remains hidden in the name Allah

Frankly speaking, to discuss the God of Islam without mentioning the name Allah would be like teaching a language without teaching its alphabet. Or it will be like smelling a rose without having its fragrance. To all Muslims, the name Allah itself is the touchstone of their faith without which its' true essence or spirit could never be felt or understood. They also claim the key to man's salvation has remained hidden in the name Allah. Let me explain in brief why they claim so.

I have borrowed this explanation mostly from The Concise Encyclopedia of Islam by Cyril Glasse, page 37. The mystery or the worth of this unique Arabic name Allah lies in the name itself as well as in its invocation. The name Allah is spelled with four Arabic letters alif, laam, laam, and haa. Let us see what comes out after we separate the letters from the name one by one.

In Arabic, the name Allah begins with its first letter Alif, which also looks like the Arabic first numeral one representing, undoubtedly of His being the First and the One.

Now, if we remove the first letter alif from the name Allah, the remaining letters will be read in Arabic as Lillah, meaning toward Allah or for the sake of Allah.

If the second letter, which is the first laam is removed, it will be read in Arabic as Lahu meaning to Him.

Then if we remove the third letter, which is the second laam, the only letter that remains is Ha, which, vocalized, becomes Huwa meaning He-the name of the Essence referring again to none but God Himself

Interestingly, when a man invokes the name Allah, its form gradually melts into breath itself. The same thing happens to the dying man whose soul is resolved into breathing alone and leaves the body through its last breath. In this way, the name Allah remains with men until their last breath, reminding them constantly of His being their One and Only Lord, Guide, Provider, Protector as well as their Ultimate Refuge.

Reverend, what I said so far with evidence and explanation, might help you and my other readers to know and understand about the God of Islam and why the Muslims regard the name "Allah" to be more appropriate to invoke or to worship, than God or His other familiar names.

Last of all, I also like to inform you that besides the name Allah, the Quran has also described many of His beautiful names denoting His unique essence and attributes through His last Prophet Muhammad. I intend to narrate some of them in the next chapter so that you and your people understand what kind of God the Muslims really adore, obey and worship.

> *And to Allah belong the most beautiful names. So, invoke Him by them. But shun those who practice deviation concerning His names....*
> *(7:180)*

Letter 2

The Quran Says God Is One and Only

Your God is One God; there is no one worthy of worship except Him, the Compassionate, the Merciful.

—Quran 2:163

Reverend,

In this letter, I intend to tell about Allah, or the God of Islam as He has described Himself in the Quran through His last and final Prophet Muhammad. There are countless verses in the Quran in which God makes Himself known to mankind through some of His unique essence and attributes. I hope this will help you and my other readers to know clearly and correctly what kind of God the Muslims really worship, adore, and obey. Before I start, I need to mention two things related to the meaning and the interpretation of the Quran for them who never read any of its verses before.

First, except for the Quran in Arabic text, which God sent to Prophet Muhammad through His Angel Gabriel, the Muslims do not regard its meaning, translation, or interpretation in other languages as the revealed Book of God. They mention those books as the meaning of the Quran in English, French, etc.

Second, the Quran has 114 Suras, or Chapters, consisting verses of unequal length. The readers need to remember the number of the Chapter is placed first, followed by the number of the verse or verses. For example, the numbers in the parenthesis (14:31-34) indicate verses 31 to 34 have been quoted from the chapter 14, the title of which is Ibrahim (Abraham).

With this little note of information, I would like to draw your attention to the translation or the meaning of the following verses of the Quran where God of Islam has made Himself and the basic truth of His guidance, known to the people through His last Prophet Muhammad about fourteen hundred years ago.

God Is One and without Any Partner

(3:18) *Allah Himself has testified to the fact that there is no God but Him and so do the angels and those who are well grounded in knowledge standing firm on justice. There is no God except Him, the Mighty, the Wise.*

(112:1–4) *[To Muhammad] Say: He is Allah, The One and Only. Allah, The Eternal, The Absolute; He begets not, nor is He begotten; and there is none comparable to Him.*

(55:26–27) *All that exists on the earth will perish, but the Face of your Lord will remain full of Majesty and Glory.*

(14:52) *This is a Message for the mankind: let them take warning from that and let them know that He is the One and Only God: and let the men of understanding take heed.*

(7:158) *[To Muhammad] Say: O mankind! I am the Messenger of Allah towards all of you from Him to whom belongs the kingdom of the heavens and the earth. There is no God but Him.*

(59:22–24) *Allah is He, beside Him there is no other god, The Knower of all things both secret and open. He is Most Gracious, Most Merciful. Allah is He, besides Him there is no other god. The Sovereign, the Holy One, the Source of Peace, the Guardian of Faith, The Preserver of Security, the Exalted in Might, the Irresistible, the Supreme: Glory be to Allah! High is He above the partners they ascribe to Him. He is Allah, the Creator, the Evolver, the Modeler to whom belong the Most Beautiful Names: All that is in the heavens and the earth declare His glory: And He is the All-Mighty, the All-Wise.*

(3:2–3) *Allah, there is no god but Him; The Living, The Eternal. He has revealed to you this Book [the Quran] with the Truth, confirming the scripture which preceded it, as He revealed the Torah and the Gospel before this.*

There are many oft-repeated verses in the Holy Quran like the last one I quoted above tell us clearly and categorically that the Holy Bible including both its Parts, carry the same eternal truth about God's being One and no one is worthy of worship besides Him. We shall check the truth in the next chapter from both parts of the Bible.

God is Omnipotent and Omniscient

(2:255) *Allah, there is no god but Him: the Living, the Eternal. Neither slumbers nor sleep overtakes Him. To Him belongs all that is in the heavens and in the earth. Who is he that can intercede with Him without His permission? He knows what is before them and what is behind them. And they encompass nothing of His knowledge except what He pleases. His throne extends over the heavens and the earth, and He feels no fatigue in preserving them. And He is the Most High, the Supreme.*

(6:59) *He Alone has the keys of the unforeseen treasures, of which no one knows except Him. He knows whatever is in the land and in the sea; there is not a single leaf that falls without His knowledge, there is neither a grain in the darkness of the earth nor anything fresh or dry but is written in a Clear Record.*

> By this clear record, the Quran refers to *al-Lawh al-Mahfuz*, meaning the guarded tablet, or the Glorious Book, which has recorded everything that exists in the entire heavens and earth, and every event that has taken place or would take place from the beginning to the day of resurrection manifesting God's overall knowledge and authority over them. It is also called the Mother Book.

6:102–103) *No vision can grasp Him while He grasps all visions. He is the Subtle, the Aware.*

(34:2) *He has the knowledge of all that goes into the earth and that which comes out of it; and all of that which comes down from heaven and that ascends to it.*

(65:12) *God is He Who has created seven Firmaments and of the earth a similar number. His Command descends through them: that you may know Allah has power over all things, and Allah comprehends all things in His knowledge.*

God is the Creator of the Entire Heavens and Earth

In the following verses of the Quran, God describes Himself as the Creator of the entire heavens and earth and everything that comes in between.

(6:1–2) All praises be to Allah, the One Who has created the heavens and the earth and made the darkness and the light; yet the unbelievers set up equal partners with their Lord. He is the One Who has created you from clay, then decreed a fixed term of life and set a deadline for you Himself; yet you go on doubting!

(13:2-3) Allah is the One Who raised the heavens without any pillars that you can see, then firmly established Him on the throne of authority and subjected the sun and the moon to His Law, each one pursuing its course for an appointed time. He regulates all affairs. He has spelled out His revelations so that you may believe in meeting your Lord.

He is the One Who spread out the earth and placed thereon mountains and rivers, created fruits of every kind in pairs, two and two, and makes the night cover the day. Certainly, in these things there are signs for those who use their common sense.

(30:19) He brings out the living from the dead and the dead from the Living and gives life to the earth after its death. Likewise, you shall be brought forth to life after your death.

(36:82) Verily, whenever He intends doing a thing, He says to it "Be" and it is!

God is the Planner and the Controller of Everything in the Universe

(13:41) The sun runs its course which is predetermined by the Almighty, the All-Knowing. As for the moon, We have designed phases for it till it again becomes like an old dry palm branch. Neither it is possible for the sun to overtake the moon, nor for the night to outstrip the day. Each float along in its own orbit (According to the Law of God). When Allah commands, there is none to reverse His Command and He is swift in taking accountability. Allah is the Master of all planning. He knows the actions of every soul.

(39:62) Allah is the creator of all things and He is the Guardian and Disposer of all affairs.

(22:66) He is the One Who has given you life, will cause you to die and then will bring you back to life again.

God Is the Provider and the Sustainer of All Living Beings

In the following verses of the Quran, we shall see that God of Islam is not only the Creator, Controller or the Master of all planning He is also the Provider and the Sustainer of every living thing that exists on, above, or beneath the earth.

(15:19–20) We have spread out the earth and set mountains upon it and caused to grow therein every suitable thing in due proportion. And We have provided therein means of subsistence for you and for those whom you do not provide.

(15:22) We send the fertilizing winds and send down water from the sky for you to drink; and it is not you who own the storage of this wealth.

(80:24–32) Let man reflect on the food he eats, how We pour down rainwater in abundance and cleave the soil asunder. How We bring forth grain, grapes and nutritious vegetation, olives and dates, lush gardens, fruit and fodder, as a mean of sustenance for you and for your cattle.

(29:60) How many a creature carries not its own provision! Allah provides for it and for you.

God's Favors to Mankind Are Beyond Any Measure

There are numerous verses in the Quran which tell us God's favors to mankind are beyond any measure. Out of many I have quoted below only a few of them.

(16:78) Allah brought you forth from the wombs of your mothers when you knew nothing, and He gave you hearing, sight and intelligence so that you might give thanks to Allah.

(14:32-34) It is Allah Who has created the heavens and the earth. He sends down rain from the sky with which He brings forth fruits for your sustenance. He has made the ships subservient to you, which may sail through

the sea by His Command; and likewise, the rivers are made for your benefit. The sun and the moon are also assigned for your benefit, which diligently pursue their courses to cause the night and day for your service. He has given you all that you could ask for and if you want to count the favors of Allah, you will never be able to count them.

(10:5) *It is He who made the sun to be a shining glory and the moon to be a light, and measured out stages for her so that you may know the number of years and the count of time. Allah created them only to manifest the truth. He has spelled out His revelations for people who want to know.*

(45:13) *He has also subjected to you whatever is in between the heavens and the earth: it is all as a favor and kindness from Him. Verily, there are signs in it for those who reflect.*

(4:10) *If anyone does evil or wrongs his own soul but afterwards seeks forgiveness, he will find Allah most Forgiving, Most Merciful.*

(39:53) *Allah says: O my servants, who have transgressed against their souls, do not despair of the mercy of Allah, for Allah forgives all sins. Truly, He is Oft-Forgiving, Most Merciful.*

No One Is Worthy of Worship besides God

Reverend, the verses I quoted above are sufficient to know and realize that God alone has the right to be worshiped since no one in the entire heavens and earth could be His equal or worthy of worship besides Him. I have quoted below a few more verses from the Quran with the same eternal message that Muhammad-the Prophet of Islam received from God and preached and practiced himself following the footsteps of all his predecessors.

(18:110) *O Muhammad, tell them: I am but a human being like you; the revelation is sent to me to declare that your God is One God; therefore, whoever hopes to meet his Lord, let him do good deeds and join no partner in the worship of his Lord.*

(28:88) *Invoke no other god besides Allah. There is no god besides Him. Everything is perishable except Him. To Him belongs the judgment and to Him you will be returned.*

(39:65–66) [To Muhammad] Say: *O ignorant! Do you bid me to worship someone other than Allah? But it has already been revealed to you as it was revealed to those before you that if you ascribe a partner to Allah, all your deeds will go in vain and you will surely be among the losers. Therefore, to worship Allah and be among His thankful servants.*

(40:66) *O Prophet, tell them: 'I have been forbidden to invoke them who you invoke besides Allah. How could I do so after clear revelations came to me from my Lord and I have commanded to submit myself to the Lord of the worlds?*

(2:21–22) *O mankind! Worship your Lord Who created you and created those who came before you. He has made the earth your couch, and the sky your canopy, and sent down rain from the heavens; and brought forth therewith fruits for your sustenance; Then do not set up rivals unto Allah [in worship] when you know the truth [that He alone has the right to be worshipped]*

Based on the above verses of the Quran, the Muslim or the followers of Muhammad, believe undoubtedly that there is none but Allah/God, Whose glory and greatness, wisdom and authority, compassion and kindness, and favors and forgiveness are beyond any measure, and therefore, none has the right to be worshiped except Him. As a Muslim, I like to admit happily and gratefully that this is Allah-the God of Islam whom we worship and obey as our Creator, Provider, Protector, Guide and Ultimate Refuge and seek for His love, mercy, forgiveness and guidance in every walk of our life.

> *He is the Lord of the heavens and the earth and of all that lies in between, so worship Him and be steadfast in His worship.*
> *Do you know of anyone who is similar to Him?*
> *(Holy Quran 19:65).*

Letter 3

Both Parts of the Holy Bible Proclaim: God Is One and Only

Hear, O Israel: The Lord our God is one Lord. And thou shalt love the Lord thy God with all thine heart, and with all thy soul, and with all thy might.

—Deuteronomy 6:4–5

Reverend,

In my last letter, I have described what the Holy Quran says about God and the basic truth of His guidance. The Quran also confirms that the Torah (Old Testament) and the Injeel (the Gospel of Jesus) contain the same eternal truth of God's being One and worship none but Him. I have quoted below a series of evidence from both parts of the Bible in support of that.

Men Knew God as Their Only Lord from the Beginning of Their Existence

We may start with Genesis, the first book of the Old Testament
(Genesis 1:1) *In the beginning, God created the heavens and the earth.*

(Genesis 2:7) *And the LORD God formed man of the dust of the ground and breathed into his nostrils the breath of life; and man became a living soul.*

(Genesis 6:8–9) *But Noah found grace in the eyes of the LORD. These are the generations of Noah: Noah was a just man and perfect in his generations, and Noah walked with God.*

The first two verses confirm that no one existed in the beginning except God Who created heaven and earth and also formed Adam-the father of mankind with dust and made him a complete human being after He breathed His spirit through his nostrils.

The last verse tells us that the path of God was defined from the start and spread of human habitation, but it was followed only by just and righteous persons like Noah.

Everlasting covenant of God made with Abraham and his seeds

In the following verses of the Genesis, we shall see Abraham and his descendants also worshipped the same one God of Adam and Noah and tried to live their lives by His commands.

(Genesis 17:1) *And when Abram [Abraham] was ninety years old and nine, the LORD appeared to Abram, and said unto him, I am the Almighty God; walk before me, and be thou perfect.*

(Genesis 17:7) *And I will establish my covenant between me and thee and thy seed after thee in their generations for an everlasting covenant, to be a God unto thee, and to thy seed after thee.*

Reverend, kindly remember this everlasting covenant of God, which He meant to be obeyed and observed by Abraham and by all his descendants. The Muslims call it "Tawhid" (in Arabic), the exact meaning of which is Islamic monotheism where God is claimed to be One and Only and none has the right to be worshipped except Him. It is in fact, the fundamental truth in the guidance of God that He revealed to all His messengers including both Jesus and Muhammad. I shall try to justify my point with other statements of the Old Testament as we proceed. Let us begin first with Moses- a mighty messenger of God as well as one of the founding pillars of the Judeo-Christian Faith. He arrived from the line of Isaac-the promised son of Abraham through his barren wife Sarah.

Moses was sent to proclaim the worship of One God and to establish His command

In the following verses of the Old Testament, God introduces Himself to Moses along with some instruction for the guidance of his people.

(Exodus 6:2–3) *And God spoke unto Moses, and said unto him, I am the LORD: And I appeared unto Abraham, unto Isaac, and unto Jacob, by the name of God Almighty, but by my name Jehovah was I not known to them.*

(Exodus 15:11) *Who is like unto thee, O LORD among the gods? Who is like thee, glorious in holiness, fearful in praises, doing wonders?*

(Exodus 15:18) *The LORD shall reign forever and ever.*

(Exodus 20:1–4) *And God spoke all these words saying, I am the LORD thy God, which have brought thee out of the land of Egypt, out of the house of bondage. Thou shalt have no other gods before me. Thou shalt not make unto thee any graven image, or any likeness of anything that is in heaven above, or that is in the earth beneath, or that is in the water under the earth.*

(Leviticus 18:4) *Ye shall do my judgments, and keep mine ordinances, to walk therein: I am the LORD your God.*

(Deuteronomy 4:39) *Know therefore this day, and consider it in thine heart, that the LORD he is God in heaven above, and upon the earth beneath: there is none else.*

We certainly do not need any explanation to understand the message of those verses I quoted above. All of them remind us repeatedly that God is One and there is none in the entire heavens and earth who is worthy of worship beside Him. I already mentioned before that it is the eternal truth in the everlasting covenant of God that He made with Abraham and with all his seeds after him (Genesis 17:7). In the following verses of the Old Testament, Moses-the mighty Prophet from the House of Israel is seen pleading his people to obey God and not to disobey Him.

(Deuteronomy 6:4–5) *Hear, O Israel: The LORD our God is one LORD. And thou shalt love the LORD thy God with all thine heart, and with all thy soul, and with all thy might.*

(Deuteronomy 6:17) *Ye shall diligently keep the commandments of the LORD your God, and His testimonies, and His statutes, which He hath commanded thee.*

(Deuteronomy 8:19) *If you ever forget the LORD your God and follow other gods and worship and bow down to them, I testify against you today that you will surely be destroyed.*

(Deuteronomy 11:26–28) *See, I am setting before you today a blessing and a curse-the blessing if you obey the commands of the LORD your God that*

I am giving you today: the curse if you disobey the commands of the LORD your God and turn from the way that I command you today by following other gods, which you have not known.

The message of the above verses is plain and simple. Like all his predecessors, Moses was also sent to teach his people to worship none but One God and to remind them of His reward and blessing, if they obeyed His commands; and of His curse and punishment, if they disobeyed Him.

David surrendered himself completely to the will and command of God

David-a mighty king and a Prophet of God from the House of Israel is also known to surrender himself completely to the will and command of God. In the following verses of the Old Testament, David expressed his unconditional love, devotion and gratitude in appreciation of His endless glory and greatness, compassion and kindness and also for His being the only True Guide, Savior and Refuge to him.

(2 Samuel 7:22) *How great you are, Sovereign LORD! There is no one like you, and there is no God but you, as we have heard with our own ears.*

(2 Samuel 22:2-3) *He (David) said: The LORD is my rock, my fortress, and my deliverer; my God is my rock, in Him I take refuge, my shield and the horn of my salvation. He is my stronghold, my refuge, and my savior ....*

(1 Chronicles 29:11–12) *Thine, O LORD, is the greatness, and the power, and the glory, and the victory, and the majesty: for all that is in the heaven and in the earth is thine; thine is the kingdom, O LORD, and thou art exalted as head above all. Both riches and honor come of thee, and thou reign over all; and in thine hand is power and might, and in thine hand it is to make great, and to give strength unto all.*

In 1Kings 2:3, we find David to advise his son Solomon from his deathbed, as did Moses to his people: *And observe what the LORD your God requires: Walk in obedience to him, and keep his decrees and commands, his laws, and regulations, as written in the Law of Moses. Do this so that you may prosper in all you do, and wherever you go.*

Solomon also followed the footsteps of his noble father David

Solomon also followed the footsteps of his noble father David. He also dedicated himself completely to establish the worship of One True God among his people and tried to do everything for His pleasure.

I have quoted below few verses from the Old Testament to justify my point.

(2 Chronicles 2:5-6) *And the house which I build is great: for great is our God above all gods. But who is able to build Him a house, seeing the heaven and heaven of heavens cannot contain Him?*

When a small scaffold was made Solomon stood upon it and knelt down upon his knees before all the congregation of Israel. Then he spread forth his hands towards heaven and said to God most humbly,

(2 Chronicles 6:14) *O LORD God of Israel, there is no God like you in the heaven, or in the earth-you who keep your covenant of love with your servants who continue wholeheartedly in your way...*

God as described in other Books of the Old Testament

The verses that I have quoted below from different Books of the Old Testament also tell us that other prophets after Solomon also arrived declaring God as their only Lord and Savior.

(Nehemiah 9:6) *You alone are the LORD, you made the heavens, even the highest heavens, and all their starry host, the earth and all that is on it, the seas and all that is in them. You give life to everything, and the multitudes of heaven worship you.*

(Psalms 86:8-10) *Among the gods there is none like you, Lord; no deeds can compare with yours. All the nations you have made will come and worship before you, Lord! they will bring glory to your name. For you are great and do marvelous deeds; you alone are God.*

(Isaiah 43:11) *I, even I, am the LORD; and besides me there is no savior.*

(Isaiah 45:21) *Declare what is to be, present it-let them take counsel together. Who foretold this long ago, who declared it from the long past? Was it not I, the LORD? And there is no God apart from me; a righteous God and a Savior; there is none but me.*

(Isaiah 46:9) *Remember the former things of old: for I am God, and there is none else; I am God, and there is none like me.*

(Jeremiah 10:10) *But the LORD is the true God, he is the living God, and an everlasting king: at his wrath the earth shall tremble, and the nations shall not be able to abide his indignation.*

(Jeremiah 25:6) *And, go not after other gods to serve them, and to worship them, and provoke me not to anger with the works of your hands; and I will do you no hurt.*

(Daniel 9:9) *To the LORD our God belong mercies and forgiveness, though we have rebelled against him.*

Men were asked to be prudent in choosing the path of God

In the following verses of the Old Testament, men were asked to be prudent and wise in pursuing their paths that could help them to fulfill the purpose of their worldly life and return to God-their Ultimate Refuge safely. God wanted them to think deeply upon the manifestation of His power, wisdom, knowledge and glory and also of His endless love, mercy, compassion and favors to them that they find in their own self and in His numerous creations in, around and above them. They were also asked to use their own intelligence and common sense to know and understand why they should choose and follow the Path of God that He showed to them from time to time through their respective messengers.

(Hosea 14:9) *Who is wise, and he shall understand these things? Prudent, and he shall know them? For the ways of the LORD are right, and the just shall walk in them: but the transgressors shall fall therein.*

(Joel 2:12–13) *Even now, declares the LORD, return to me with all your heart, with fasting and weeping, and mourning: Rend your heart and not your garments. Return to the LORD your God, for he is gracious and compassionate, slow to anger, and abounding in love……*

Reverend, the message of the verses that I quoted so far from different parts of the Old Testament is clear and conclusive. It is, God is One and people should worship Him alone as their only Lord and Savior. I don't think any more explanation is required to convince you that all the recognized messengers of God who were sent before Jesus for the guidance of their people, conveyed the same message about God regardless to their time and place. So did Jesus-the illustrious son of Mary, when God sent him last from the House of Israel for the guidance of his own people-the misguided Jews.

God as described in the Gospel of Jesus

Reverend, in many places of the Quran, we have been told repeatedly that Jesus whom we love and respect dearly as a mighty messenger of God, was also sent following the footsteps of all his predecessors. (5:46) In other word, Jesus also called his people to worship none but One God and to strive for their eternal life through keeping His commands as did David and Moses, and other prophets before him. Similarly, the Gospel of Jesus which you believe absolutely as the true account of Jesus' own words and deeds, also tells us clearly about One True God and to worship none but Him. I think the following statements of Jesus will be enough to verify the truth.

(Mark 12:29–30)) *And Jesus answered him [a Jewish scribe], The first of all the commandments is, Hear, O Israel, the LORD our GOD is ONE LORD: And thou shalt love the LORD thy GOD with all thy heart, and with all thy soul, and with all thy mind and with all thy strength: this is the first commandment.*

(Matthew 4:10) *In reply to all the lucrative offers of the Satan (Matthew 4:8-9), Jesus said to him in disgust, "Get thee hence, Satan: for it is written, THOU SHALT WORSHIP THE LORD THY GOD, AND HIM ONLY SHALT THOU SERVE.*

Jesus says, God Alone is all Perfect

(Matthew 19:16–17) *And behold, one came and said unto him [to Jesus], Good Master, what good thing shall I do, that I may have eternal life? And he said unto him, Why callest thou me good? There is none good but one, that is, God: but if thou wilt enter into life, keep the commandments.*

By this advice to the young man, Jesus made it absolutely clear that God alone is all perfect and to have an eternal life, people must live their lives by His commands that He revealed to them from time to time through their respective messengers.

Jesus' clear view in keeping the commands of God

(Matthew 5:17–19) *Do not think that I have come to abolish the Law or the prophets; I have not come to abolish them but to fulfill them. For truly I tell you, until heaven and earth disappear, not the smallest letter, not the least stroke of a pen, will by any means disappear from the Law until everything is accomplished. Therefore, anyone who sets aside one of the least of these commandments and teaches others accordingly, will be called least in the kingdom of heaven, but whoever practices and teaches these commands will be called great in the kingdom of heaven.*

By those commands, Jesus obviously meant the Laws of the Torah which God revealed to Moses for the guidance of his people. In other word, Jesus did not arrive with any new law, he arrived to implement the Laws of the Torah among his people who deviated from it.

Similarly, Muhammad whom God sent after Jesus, also tried to teach his people to worship none but One True God and to strive for their eternal life through keeping His commands as did all his predecessors before him. We shall check the truth in the next chapter.

> *To every messenger whom We sent before you (Muhammad), We revealed the same message: "There is no God but Me, so worship Me Alone."*
> (Quran 21:25)

Letter 4

Muhammad Was Sent after Jesus Reviving, and Restoring Abraham's Faith, in Islam

Say (O Muhammad): we believe in God and in what has been revealed to us, and what was sent down to Abraham, Ishmael, Isaac, Jacob their descendants; and what was given to Moses, Jesus and other prophets from their Lord; We make no distinction between one another among them, and we submit to God as Muslim.

—Holy Quran 3:84

Reverend,

From the description of my last two letters you certainly have noticed that God's guidance for mankind which He revealed through all His messengers including both Jesus and Muhammad, had one thing in common. It is pure and pristine monotheism-the basic truth in His guidance. Abraham received it through the everlasting covenant of God while Moses and Jesus received it through His First Commandment. Muhammad-the last of them is also known to receive the same message from God in Islam-the latest of all His religions. It is called Tawhid in Arabic and it has been translated in English as 'Islamic monotheism' because Islam is the only religion on earth where pure monotheism in the guidance of God has remained intact until now.

According to *Merriam-Webster's Encyclopedia of World Religions* (page 747), "Islamic monotheism is more literal and uncompromising than that of any other religion. Allah is confessed as being one, eternal, unbegotten, unequaled, and beyond partnership of any kind."

God has chosen the name "Islam" for His religion and "Muslim" for its adherents

The Quran tells us God has chosen the name "Islam" for His religion and "Muslim" for its adherents. (5:3; 3:19; 22:78, 42:13). Both the names have been originated from *salaam* in Arabic, which ordinarily means peace or submission for Islam, and calm or submissive for Muslim. But in a broader sense, Islam means a complete surrender or resignation to the will and the command of God. Similarly, Muslim refers to a person who submits to God completely while striving for His cause and seeking for His pleasure. (3:19- 20, 83–85).

In that sense, all the messengers of God before Muhammad were Muslims and what they preached and practiced in His name, was Islam. In my last two letters, I have provided plenty of clear evidence from both our Holy Scriptures-the Quran and the Bible in support of that. I shall now try to provide more evidence from the Quran to establish Muhammad's role and mission as the last Prophet and the last Reminder of God's guidance for mankind that He sent through all His messengers before him.

God's guidance for mankind began with Adam and Eve in heaven

The story of Adam and Eve has been told and retold in many places of the Quran where we have learnt how God made them in heaven and how they were deceived by the Satan and ate the forbidden fruit by disobeying the command of God. We also learned God forgave them both when they repented sincerely for their disobedience to Him. Then according to the Preset timetable of God, they were sent down to earth along with the Satan as their open enemy. The Quran tells us God sent them to earth along with His guidance where He said:

Get down from here all of you. Henceforth, there shall come to you guidance from Me, those who accept and follow it, shall have nothing to fear or to regret. But those who reject and defy Our revelation, will be inmates of hellfire, wherein they shall live forever (2:38–39).

God also said to the Satan separately: *Get out from here, you despicable outcast; I will certainly fill hell with you and all of them who follow you (7:18)*.

The Quran also tells us repeatedly the bottom line in God's guidance to Adam, has remained the same in the teaching of all His prophets including both Jesus and Muhammad. All of them conveyed to their people that they would return to God-their Ultimate Refuge safely if they follow His Commands, but they would be punished in hellfire, if they disobey Him and follow the path of the Satan. We shall now check the truth in the teaching of all the prophets of God who were sent after Adam for the guidance of their people.

Noah and other prophets of God as described in the Quran

God made their role and mission known to us through His last Prophet Muhammad.

(7:59) *We sent Noah to his people. He said: O my people, worship Allah! You have no other god but Him. I fear for you the punishment of a dreadful day!*

(37:123–126) *Elias was surely one of the messengers. "Behold, he said to his people: "Have you no fear of Allah? Would you invoke Bal, (the name of their invented god) and forsake the best of the Creators-Allah Who is your Lord and the Lord of your forefathers?"*

(11:50) *To the people of Ad We sent their brother Hud. He said: "O my people! Worship Allah, you have no other god but Him. You are not but the inventors of falsehood."*

(11:61) *To the tribe of Thamud, We sent their brother Salih. He said, "O my people! Worship Allah: You have no other god but Him. It is He Who created you from the earth and made you dwell on it. So, seek forgiveness from Him and turn to Him in repentance. Surely, my Lord is near, and respond to sincere prayer."*

(29:36) *To the people of Median We sent their brother Shuaib who said, "O my people! Worship Allah, and look forward to the Last Day, and do not transgress in the land wickedly."*

Abraham-a great advocate and the upholder of pure and pristine monotheism

In the Quran, Abraham is frequently addressed as Hanif, meaning the upright and the upholder of pure and pristine monotheism. Though he was born and brought up in a pagan society, he did not fail to recognize the existence of one true eternal God, His absolute power and wisdom. (6:79) When his people started arguing with him, he said to them: *Will you argue with me about Allah when He has guided me Himself? I do not fear those whom you worship in association with Allah. Nothing can happen to me unless it is so willed by my Lord. The knowledge of my Lord encompasses all things. Will you not then admonish yourself?*

(60:4) *You have an excellent example in Abraham and in his companions. They said to their people straight: We are clear of you and whatever you worship besides Allah. We renounce you, and hostility and hatred shall reign forever in between us until you believe in Allah and Him alone.*

Abraham's descendants also followed the legacy of his faith

(2:132) *This is the legacy that Abraham left to his sons. So did Jacob when he said: O my sons! God has chosen for you this Deen, therefore, die not unless you are Muslims.*

> 'Deen is an Arabic term with a complex meaning. In general, it means religion, a way of life, a set rule or instruction that God has prescribed for the guidance of the people through their respective messengers.

(2:133) [To Muhammad] *Were you present when death approached Jacob? He asked his sons: Who will you worship after me? They replied: We will worship the same One God Who is your Lord and the Lord of your forefathers Abraham, Ishmael, and Isaac, and to Him we have surrendered [as Muslims].*

(6:85–87) *We gave him [Abraham] Isaac and Jacob and guided them all as we guided Noah before them, and among his descendants were David, Solomon, Job, Joseph, Moses and Aaron; thus We reward those who do good to others.*

Other descendants include Zechariah, John, Jesus, and Elias; all of them were righteous; and Ishmael, Elisha, Jonah, and Lot. We exalted each of them over the mankind. And we exalted some of their forefathers, their children, and their brothers. We chose them for Our service and guided them to the Right Path.

Joseph- great-grandson of Abraham also advised his people to worship none but One God

(12:38–40) [Joseph says to the fellow-prisoners,] *"I follow the ways of my fathers-Abraham, Isaac and Jacob; and it is never for us to associate any partner to Allah: This is Allah's favors upon us and to mankind; but most men are not grateful.*

"O my two companions of the prison! Are many lords differing among themselves better or One Allah, Supreme and Irresistible?

"Those whom you worship beside Him, are but names that you or your forefathers have invented, for which Allah has provided you no authority. It is none but Allah Who gives the Command. He has commanded that you worship none but Him: This is the right religion, but most men understand not."

Moses was sent to proclaim the worship of One God among his people

In the following verses of the Quran, we shall check what Moses, the mighty messenger of God from the House of Israel and one of the Founder-Pillars of the Judeo-Christian faith, has received from God for the guidance of his people.

(17:2) *We gave Moses the Book [Torah] and made it a guide to the children of Israel commanding: Take not, other but Me as the Disposer of your affairs.*

(20:13–15) [To Moses] *I have chosen you: so, listen to what I reveal to you.*

Verily, I am Allah. There is no God but Me. So, worship Me alone and establish regular prayer for my remembrance.

The final Hour is sure to come. But I will keep it hidden, so that every soul may be rewarded according to its efforts.

(21:48) *Certainly, We granted to Moses and Aaron the Criterion of right and wrong, a light and a reminder for those people who are righteous.*

(20:97) *Then he [Moses] addressed his people saying, O my people! Your only God is Allah. There is no other God besides Him. His knowledge encompasses everything.*

David surrendered himself completely for the Cause of God

There are many verses in the Quran where Muhammad is reminded of David's unconditional love, longing, and complete submission to God and how his Almighty and Merciful Lord rewarded him for that.

(38:17-20) *O Prophet! Bear with what they (who rejected Muhammad's call to Islam) say, and remember Our servant David, the man of strength. Verily, he was ever turning in repentance towards Allah.*

We made the mountains to join him in Our praises at evening and in the morning.

And the birds, too, joined him in flocks to sing with him.

We strengthened his kingdom and gave him wisdom and sound judgment.

His son Solomon also showed his complete allegiance to the will and command of God

(27:15) *We gave knowledge to David and Solomon: and they both said: Praise be to Allah Who has favored us above many of His believing servants.*

(38:35-36) *He [Solomon] said: O my Lord! Forgive me and grant me a kingdom similar of which does not belong to any one after me. Surely, you are the Giver without any measure. So, We subjected to him the wind that blew gently to whichever direction he wanted.*

Reverend, the contents of the above-quoted verses tell us clearly that David and his son Solomon also worshipped the same One God and followed His commands as did His other prophets before them.

So did Jesus-the noble, chaste and the righteous son of Mary whom God sent last from the House of Israel for the guidance of his own people-the misguided Jews.

Jesus-the last Prophet from the House of Israel also asked his people to worship God alone

Reverend, the Quran gives an extra coverage on Mary and especially on her son Jesus, to clarify their true status to the Christians and the non-Christians both. The Muslims have learnt from the Quran about his miraculous birth, miracles he performed, his mysterious death on the

Cross, his ascent to heaven alive, his Second Coming, and above all, what he taught to his people in the name of God and what he never taught. The Quran also tells us that Jesus- the last Prophet of God from the House of Israel and the other indispensable name related to the Judeo-Christian faith, also guided his people to the Path of God following the footsteps of their Predecessors. I have quoted below only a few of them to justify my claim.

(5:46) Then, in the footsteps of those prophets, We sent Jesus, the son of Mary, confirming the Law [Torah] that had come before him: And We sent him the Gospel where there was guidance and light and confirmation of the Torah which was sent before him; a guidance and admonition to those who fear Allah. [ref: Matthew 5:17-19]

(5:72) Surely, they have disbelieved who say: God is the Messiah [Jesus] son of Mary. While Christ said himself, O children of Israel! Worship God, My Lord, and your Lord.

(3:50)) I, (Jesus) am appointed to confirm the Law which was before me and to make lawful some of that which was forbidden to you. I have come to you with a sign from your Lord, so fear Allah, and obey me.

Muhammad arrived last confirming the worship of the same One God of all his predecessors

Reverend, there are many oft-repeated verses in the Quran which tell us Muhammad- the last and the final Messenger of God was also sent proclaiming the worship of the same One God of all his predecessors. Out of many, I have quoted below only a few of them.

Say (O Muhammad!) we believe in God and in what has been revealed to us, and what was sent down to Abraham, Ishmael, Isaac, Jacob and their descendants; and what was given to Moses, Jesus and other prophets from their Lord; We make no distinction between one another among them, and we submit to God as Muslim (3:84).

O Muhammad! We have sent revelations to you just as We sent to Noah, and the Prophets who came after him; We also sent revelations to Abraham, Ishmael, Isaac, Jacob, his descendants, Jesus, Job, Jonah, Aaron and Solomon, and to David We gave the Psalms. Revelations were also sent to those Messengers whom We have mentioned to you and to those whose names We have not mentioned; To Moses Allah spoke directly (4:163–164).

[To Muhammad] *Say: O mankind! Verily, I am sent to you all as the messenger of God to Whom belongs the kingdom of heavens and the earth. There is no Deity but Him. It is He Who gives life and causes death. So, believe in God and His messenger, the unlettered prophet [Muhammad] who believes in God and in His words [what He revealed in the Quran, the Gospel, and the Torah]. And follow him so that you may be rightly guided.* (7:158)

The messengers of God were many, but His message was one

Reverend, you certainly have noticed by this time that the eternal truth in the guidance of God which is pure and pristine monotheism, has remained the same in the teaching of all His prophets beginning from Adam to His last Prophet Muhammad and who were sent in between them. It also reminds us clearly that the messengers of God were many, but His message that He sent through them, was one. All of them were sent to ask their people in one voice to believe in One God, to worship none but Him and to follow His commands regardless to their time. place, race, or religion. It is like the whiteness of milk that always remains the same irrespective of the color or the type of cows.

The Bible describes this eternal message of God in Isaiah 40:8, *The grass withereth, the flower fadeth: but the word of our God shall stand forever.*

Similarly, the Quran says in 17:77, *This has always been our Ways with the apostles whom We sent before you (Muhammad). You will find no change in our Ways.*

Causes of man's deviation from the Path of God

At this point, any sensible and open-minded person may ask in wonder, how could men deviate from that plain, simple, and straight path of God after it was taught by all His messengers so clearly and consistently right from the beginning? Should not they have followed the same trodden path of all His messengers instead of following so many paths which are not only different from one another but sometimes are completely reverse from the others?

In the following verses of the Quran we have been told why men derailed from that repeatedly mentioned path of God which we still find in the teaching of all His prophets whom He sent one after another for the guidance of their people.

(2:213) *Mankind was one community and Allah sent His Prophets with glad tidings and warnings, and with them He sent the Scripture with the truth to settle the matters in between them where they differed. And the very people, to whom it [the Book] was given, started disputes because of rivalry in between one another after the clear proofs had come unto them.*

(3:19) *Surely, the true religion in the sight of Allah is Islam [meaning submission to His will and command]. Those who received the Scripture before differed through envy of each other, only after true knowledge had come to them.*

(21:92–93) *Verily this brotherhood of yours is a single brotherhood and I am your only God, therefore worship Me Alone. But the people have divided their religion into sects in between them-to Us they shall all return.*

There are also numerous verses in the Quran in which men's ego, arrogance, ignorance, ingratitude, obliviousness, pride, prejudice and above all, their heedlessness and extreme love for the material world, have been blamed for their deviation from the plain, simple, and straight path of God. I have quoted some of them from different chapters of the Quran.

(10:31) [To Muhammad] *Ask them: Who provides your sustenance from the heaven and from the earth? Who has control over hearing and sight? Who brings forth the living from the dead and the dead from the living? They will soon reply Allah/God. Say: Why do you not then fear Him for your going against the truth?*

(31:25) *If you ask them who has created the heavens and the earth? They will certainly say: Allah/God. Say: Praise be to Allah! But the fact is, most of them do not use their common sense to understand.*

(23:80) *It is He Who gives life and causes you die, and in His control is the alternation of the night and day: then why don't you understand?*

(10:36) *The fact is that most of them follow nothing, but mere conjecture and conjecture is no way a substitute for the truth. Surely Allah/God is well-aware of what they do.*

(7:179) *Those are the ones who have hearts with which they do not understand, they have eyes with which they do not see, they have ears with which they do not hear. They are like animals even worse than them because they are those who are heedless.*

Muhammad was sent last reviving, rectifying, and restoring Abraham's Faith in Islam

The Quran tells us Muhammad was sent last reviving, rectifying, and restoring Abraham's faith in Islam and choosing it as the only way of life for all of mankind. The following verses of the Quran can be taken into consideration in support of that.

(42:13) *He (Allah) has ordained for you the same Deen (Islam) which He enjoined on Noah and which We have revealed to you (O Muhammad!) and which We enjoined on Abraham and Moses and Jesus: "Establish the Deen of Al-Islam and make no division in it."*

(4:125) *Who can be better in religion than a Muslim (who submits himself entirely to Allah), does good to others and follows the faith of Abraham the upright whom Allah chose to be His friend?*

(6:161–162) *Say [O Muhammad]: As for me, surely my Lord has guided me to a Straight Path, a Right Religion, the faith of Abraham, the upright and he was not of them who worshiped God in association with others. Say: Surely my prayer, my sacrifice, my life, and my death are all for Allah, the Lord of the Worlds.*

(3:67-68) *Abraham was neither a Jew nor a Christian but was a Muslim [submitted himself to the will and the command of God], true in faith. He was not one of them who set up partners with God. Surely, those of mankind who have the best claim to Abraham are those who follow him in submission to God and this Prophet [Muhammad] and those who believe with him.*

According to the quoted statements of the Quran, it is only the Muslims or the followers of the last Prophet Muhammad, have the best claim on Abraham as their Patriarch or as the inheritors to his faith. The Muslims have been claiming so for the last fourteen hundred years, because Islam is still the only religion of God where Abraham's pure monotheistic faith has remained intact or unchanged.

Muhammad arrived as the last Reminder and the Warner for all of mankind

The Quran also tells us repeatedly that Muhammad was sent as the last Reminder and the Warner for all of mankind. It is through him, God reminds them all for one last time about the glad tidings that He promised to them in return to their following His path. Similarly, it is through Muhammad God also reminds them all for one last time about the fatal consequences that they might face for their being misled from His path. I have quoted from the Quran the following statements in support of that.

(17:105) *We have revealed the Quran in Truth, and with the Truth it has come down: and We have sent you [Muhammad] as a bearer of glad tidings [to the believers] and as a warner [to the unbelievers].*

(25:56–57) *We have sent you only as a bearer of good news and a warner. Say: I ask of you of no recompense for this work except that he who wants, may choose the Right Way to His Lord.*

(38:65–68) *Say, [O Muhammad!] I am but a plain warner; and there is no Deity except Allah, the One, the Irresistible, the Lord of the heavens and the earth and all that lies in between them, the Almighty, the Forgiver. Say: This is a supreme message: yet you pay no heed to it.*

(39:64–65) *[To Muhammad] Say to them [who ascribe partnership to God]: O ignorant! Do you bid me worship someone other than Allah? And verily, it has already been revealed to you as it was revealed to those before you that if you ascribe a partner to Allah, all your deeds will go in vain and you will surely be among the losers.*

(18:110) *O Muhammad, tell them: I am but a human being like you; the revelation is sent to me to declare that your God is One God; therefore, whoever hopes to meet his Lord, let him do good deeds and join no partner in the worship of his Lord.*

(41:52) *O Prophet, ask them: Have you ever considered if this Quran is really from Allah and you deny it, who can be more astray than you who have gone too far defying Him.*

Reverend, I think the verses which I quoted before from both parts of the Bible and now from the Quran, will be enough for you to know and believe that Muhammad-the last Prophet of God was neither an imposter nor an inventor of a new faith or cult, as you and most of your people blame him, unknowingly. Rather, God has sent him last for all of mankind following the footsteps of all his predecessors and reviving and restoring their pure monotheistic faith in Islam. In that case, I don't need to provide you any further evidence to nullify your comment where you said, "The god of Islam is not the same God of the Christians or the Judeo-Christian faith. It is a different god." In that sense, I have also completed my argument and I should stop here thanking you gratefully for giving me a chance to let your people know about the God of Islam and the God of the Judeo-Christian faith as He described Himself in the Quran through His last Prophet Muhammad, as well as in both parts of the Bible through Jesus, Moses, Abraham, and other prophets whom He sent before Muhammad.

It is not the Muslims it is in fact, the Christians who worship a different God

But I could not stop, because while reading the Quran and both parts of the Bible, I came to know that it is not the Muslims, it is in fact the Christians who worship "a different god" from the God of Jesus, Moses, and Abraham. They have been doing so since they made Jesus as an Object of worship along with One True God or as one of the Gods in the Trinity. Any sensible, attentive, and open-minded reader of the Bible and Quran, will consider it as a colossal deviation from the eternal truth of the First Commandment that Jesus preached and practiced himself all through his life following the footsteps of all his Predecessors.

Reverend, it is absolutely for the sake of truth and also for our special love and respect for Jesus as a unique and special messenger of God, I wrote to you eight letters more where I've tried to explain in details who Jesus really was, why he was sent for, what he taught his people in the name of God, and what he never taught. I also tried my utmost to support my argument with clear evidence from both Parts of the Bible, the Quran, and other authentic sources

> *O Muhammad! declare: "O mankind, the truth has come to you from your Lord! He that follows guidance, does it for his own good and he that goes astray, does so at his own risk; for I am not a custodian over you."*
> *(Quran 10:108)*

Letter 5

Jesus' Comforter Is Muhammad, the Prophet of Islam

But when the Comforter is come, whom I will send unto you from the Father, even the Spirit of truth, which proceeds from the Father, he shall testify of me.

—John 15:26–27

Reverend,

You may feel surprised to know that the topic I chose for this letter is not Jesus but his Comforter, whom he mentioned in many of his predictions. Jesus told his disciples that his Comforter or the Advocate would come from God to testify of him. I chose to talk about his Comforter first, because I need his testimony to prove that Jesus was not a Deity but a mighty messenger of God, and he never taught any of those doctrines that his followers now believe in his name as the integral parts of their faith. We shall go into them one by one after we check who Jesus really meant to be his Comforter so that we could accept his testimony about him (Jesus) to be true and valid.

Jesus' Comforter is not the Holy Ghost, but Muhammad-the last Prophet of God

Following the signs or the indications in Jesus' predictions, the Muslims believe undoubtedly that his Comforter is Muhammad, the last Prophet of God, though you may nullify their claim with his another prediction in John 14:26, where he said clearly:

But the Comforter which is the Holy Ghost, whom the Father will send in my name, He shall teach you all things, and bring all things to your remembrance, whatsoever I have said unto you.

After this clear prediction, it is very much expected that you would claim Jesus' Comforter is no one else but the Holy Ghost. In reply to that, I would request you humbly to have patience with me until I prove with clear evidence from both parts of the Bible that Jesus meant none but Muhammad-the Prophet of Islam as his Comforter and Testifier both.

The Holy Ghost vs. the Holy Spirit

To verify the truth of my claim, we need to check first who was this Holy Ghost that Jesus meant for his Comforter or Testifier? To verify the truth, we should first try to know the exact meaning or implication about two translated names in the Bible: the Holy Ghost and the Holy Spirit.

Jesus used to teach his people in his native language Aramaic, which had been translated first into Hebrew, from Hebrew to Greek, and from Greek to English. As we are concerned only with the English version of the Bible, I shall explain first how the Holy Ghost came into English from the Greek version of the Bible.

The learned scholars of the Western world have detected some confusion while translating the phrase "Holy Ghost" or "Holy Spirit" from Greek to English. They found pneuma in Greek is the root word for spirit, and it has no separate word for ghost. So, in many places of the King James and Roman Catholic version of the Bible, the Holy Ghost, and the Holy Spirit both have been used to mean the same thing or to serve the same purpose.

In the Revised Standard Version of the Bible, which was reviewed and edited by some thirty-two scholars of the highest eminence and backed by fifty cooperating denominations, the word Ghost was replaced by Spirit. At this point, it is important to note that both Bible and Quran have used the term Spirit for a Messenger of God, who is usually appointed from the angels and also from humankind to carry out the command of God. Let me justify my point with some instances from our Holy Scriptures-the Bible and the Quran both.

(Luke 3:22) *And the Holy Ghost [Spirit] descended in a bodily shape like a dove upon him. [Jesus]*

(Luke 22:43) *And there appeared an angel unto him [Jesus] from the heaven, strengthening him.*

(Quran 5:110) *Then Allah will ask: O Jesus son of Mary! Recall my favor upon you and to your mother, how I strengthened you with the Holy Spirit.*

(Quran 16:102) *[To Muhammad] Say: The Holy Spirit has brought the revelation from your Lord in truth, in order to strengthen those who believe, and as a guide and glad tidings to the Muslims [who surrender to God].*

At this point, it is important to note "the Holy Spirit" refers exclusively to Angel Gabriel-the chief of all angels in both Bible and Quran. We will come to that later while explaining other prediction of Jesus about his Comforter.

The term "Spirit" has been used for both true and false prophet

We read the following statement in 1John 4:1–3

Dear friends, do not believe every spirit but test the spirits to see whether they are from God because many false prophets have gone out into the world. This is how you can recognize the Spirit of God: Every spirit that acknowledges that Jesus Christ has come in the flesh is from God, but every spirit that does not acknowledge that Jesus Christ has come in the flesh is not from God. (NIV)

In this statement, the spirit has been substituted for a prophet from humankind regardless of his status. In this precautionary note, John-a disciple of Jesus describes that no angel or a spiritual being would arrive to tell us whether Jesus came in the flesh or not. John meant a true Prophet of God from humankind would come to remind the world who Jesus really was and why he was sent for. He also pointed out how to differentiate a true prophet of God from the false one. A true prophet would never say that God appeared to them in the flesh of Jesus, but a false prophet would claim so. A true Prophet would teach Jesus was a man of flesh and blood and he was sent to his people to guide them by the command of God. It is what Muhammad did when God sent him after Jesus as his testifier. But the false prophets who arrived after Jesus taught the people that he was God Incarnate as well as one of the Gods in the Trinity, and they should worship him as God or along with God. We shall now examine the last part of Jesus' prophecy in John 14:26 to know whom he really meant to be his Advocate, Comforter, or Testifier.

He shall teach you all things and bring all things to your remembrance (John 14:26)

"He shall teach you all things and bring all things to your remembrance," describes Muhammad accurately . Being an inspired Messenger of God, Jesus knew in advance that a day would come after him, when his people would be misled by the invented doctrines of men which they would teach them in his name. He also knew God would send Muhammad after him along with His final guidebook-the Quran testifying in it of his true status and reminding his people of what he really taught them and what he never taught. To verify the truth, you may read again the last few pages of my last two letters where I mentioned about Jesus and his teaching from both Bible and Quran.

By this prediction in John 14:26, Jesus also confirmed indirectly but undoubtedly that he did not mean the Holy Ghost to be his Comforter. How could he mean the invisible Holy Ghost to appear before his people and to bring everything back to their memory through his teaching? We may now check what Jesus said about his Comforter in his other predictions.

In John 16:13-14, Jesus said to his disciples:

Howbeit when he, the Spirit of Truth, is come, he will guide you into all truth. For he shall not speak of himself; but whatsoever he shall hear that he shall speak, and he will shew you things to come. He shall glorify me: for he shall receive of mine and shall show it unto you.

Reverend, you may not like to hear it, but "The Spirit of Truth" in John 16:13 describes Muhammad accurately.

According to all his biographers, both ancient and modern, Arab, and non-Arab, Muslims and non-Muslims, Muhammad was called Al Amin (in Arabic), meaning the truthful or trustworthy by all his pagan kith and kin since his boyhood. They called him so for his being scrupulously honest, truthful, and trustworthy. In other word, Muhammad's love and commitment for truth and trustworthiness was known to all, long before he claimed himself a Prophet of God.

"He will guide you into all truth," refers to none but Prophet Muhammad

According to the description of the Holy Scriptures-the Bible and the Quran both, the eternal truth in the guidance of God, is pure and pristine monotheism. The Bible has called it the Everlasting Covenant or the First Commandment of God (Genesis 17:7; Duet 6:4-5; Mark 12:29-30). Interestingly, the Quran has not mentioned it under any special name or phrase though it tells us repeatedly the eternal truth in the guidance of God or in His religion Islam is pure and pristine monotheism. It is Muhammad-the Prophet of Islam who has called it "Tawhid" (in Arabic) the meaning of which is "Islamic Monotheism" where God is claimed to be One and none has the right to be worshiped except Him. It is like knowing the name of Alphabet after we learn the letters. The history of Christianity also tells us Jesus' true followers used to worship none but One God while he lived with them. But, after his ascent to heaven, they somehow deviated from it and began to worship God along with Jesus. Being an inspired Messenger of God, Jesus knew it was inevitable. At the same time, Jesus also knew God would send His last Messenger Muhammad to remind them about the eternal message of His guidance and to guide them back to His right path.

For he shall not speak of himself; but whatsoever he shall hear, that shall he speak (John 16:13)

Based on the well-established Islamic Tradition and Muhammad's biographies-both old and modern, we came to know he began to receive the words from God through the Angel Gabriel at the age of forty when he was meditating in the solitary cave of the Mount Hira 'near Makkah'. As he was illiterate and did not know how to read or write he had to repeat the message of God with Gabriel until he committed them by heart. Then he conveyed the same to his people as he heard and learnt from the Angel. In other word, while delivering the message of God he did not add anything to that from his own, nor he omitted or held back anything from what he learnt. The Holy Quran has still been carrying the same words as Muhammad received from God through Gabriel about fourteen hundred years ago. At this point, I also like to mention that through fulfilling this prediction of Jesus, Muhammad also fulfilled God's Promise to Moses about sending a Prophet like him in Deut. 18:18 where he said: *I will put my words in his mouth; and he shall speak unto them all that I shall command him.*

And he will show you things to come (John 16:13).

According to the description of many authentic Hadith (traditions related to Muhammad's own words and deeds as recounted by his close companions), Muhammad made a series of prophecies, including the signs of the Last Hour and of Jesus' Second Coming. Many of them occurred soon after he left, and many of them have still been occurring in and around us. Signs of his other predictions about the approach of the Last Day are also getting prominent day by day. We also believe each of his predictions mentioned in his authentic Hadith, is bound to occur by the Preset timetable of God. I like to mention only a few of them that have already occurred and are still occurring proving him to be a true Prophet of God as it is mentioned in Duet 18:22.

- Before his demise, Muhammad called his daughter Fatima to his bedside and told her she would be the first among his family to join him after his death. Fatima, who was then only twenty- eight, joined her father six months after he left.

- Muhammad predicted the caliphate (the reign of his rightly guided companions) would last for thirty years and then there would be biting kingship. The history of Islam tells us the prediction of the noble prophet came true, as he said.

- Muhammad predicted Uthman (third caliph of Islam) would be killed while reading the Quran, and so it happened

  I will quote below a few more predictions of Muhammad that he made to his people about fourteen hundred years ago, the truth of which is now more than evident.

- Muhammad said the Muslims would conquer Damascus, Jerusalem, Iraq, Persia, Constantinople, and Cyprus, and their religion Islam, would reach as far as the remotest corners of the world in the East and the West. These predictions of Muhammad not only fulfilled after he left, but they also became a part of history.

- The barefooted Bedouins would compete in building tall buildings.

- The mosques would be built like palaces.

- Killing would increase in such a way that the one who killed would not know why he killed, and the one killed would not know why he was killed.

- Sexual promiscuity would increase and a new disease, which people had not heard of before, would spread among them because of that.

- Women would appear naked while still being dressed.

- People would hop between cloud and earth. (Referring to journey by air).

"He [the Spirit of Truth] shall glorify me," matches only with Muhammad who came after Jesus

Reverend, I already explained before how the "Spirit of Truth" applies to Muhammad-the Prophet of Islam. We shall now check how Muhammad, who arrived nearly six hundred years after Jesus, glorified him. We shall find the answer in the Quran where God testified Jesus' true status and glorified him and his mother Mary through His last Prophet Muhammad. It is also with the testimony of the Quran, Jesus was made free from the accountability of those invented doctrines of men that his followers believed in his name as the integral parts of their faith after he left. (Quran 3:42–55; 4:156-157, 172; 5:46, 72–73, 116–117; 19: 27-36, 88–92; 43:59, 63–64)

Jesus' Comforter will come after he leaves is Muhammad-the Last Prophet of God

In John 16:7, Jesus said to his disciples: *Nevertheless, I tell you the truth; It is expedient for you that I go away; for if I go not away, the Comforter will not come unto you; but if I depart, I will send him unto you.*

In this prediction, Jesus made it quite clear that his Comforter would come after his departure, and not before that. So, it happened, because no other prophet of God except Muhammad came after Jesus with a revealed Book like the Quran or a great religion like Islam. The Quran also contains a prophecy of Jesus bearing the good news of Muhammad's arrival by his other name Ahmad. In the verse 61:6, God says through Muhammad:

And, remember when Jesus-the son of Mary said, O children of Israel! I am the Messenger of Allah towards you, confirming the Torah which came before me, and to give you glad tidings of a Messenger who will come after me, whose name shall be Ahmad.

By this prediction in both Bible and Quran, Jesus also confirms that he never meant the Holy Ghost or the Holy Spirit to be his Comforter, because there are many instances in both Gospel and Quran that tell us the Holy Ghost appeared to Jesus before his departure from earth. (Luke 3:21-22; Quran 5:110)

Jesus' "another Comforter," describes Muhammad-the Prophet of Islam accurately

While talking to his disciples about the Comforter, Jesus said to them, *And I will pray the Father, and he shall give you another Comforter that he may abide with you forever.* (John 14:16)

We shall first try to know what Jesus really meant by 'another Comforter?' The scholars of the Bible used the Greek word "allon" for another. It also means "another of the same kind." In that case, we can rightly assume that Jesus wanted his disciples to know and believe that his 'another Comforter' would be someone like him, having the same status or position that he had as a special Messenger of God. The Quran also tells us to believe and respect all the prophets of God equally and without making any distinction among them. (3:84) Accordingly, we believe that Jesus and Muhammad both had the same status as the true messengers of God, and both were sent to fulfill the same mission which is to establish the worship of One True God among the people and to guide them all to His path. In this connection, we should also remember that the role or the mission of the invisible Holy Spirit was completely different from Jesus' role or mission, but it was same with Prophet Muhammad, whom God sent after him fulfilling his prayer.

"He [The Comforter] may abide with you forever," matches only with last Prophet Muhammad

This last part of Jesus' prediction in John 14:16, also describes Prophet Muhammad perfectly well. Some of my missionary friends, however, wanted to know how Muhammad, who came long after Jesus with a different religion, could live forever with his followers meaning the Christians.

In reply to their question, I surprised them saying that Jesus- the last Messenger of God from the House of Israel meant the Muslims to be his true followers. Then I explained to them why or how. I told them it is only the Muslims who love and respect Jesus as a unique and special Messenger of God because of his miraculous birth, his ascent to heaven alive and of his second coming. It is only the Muslims who never believe in Jesus' deity or in the doctrine of the Trinity. It is only the Muslims who believe in the message of the First Commandment and worship none but God as their only Lord and Savior as Jesus preached and practiced himself all through his life. In that sense, it is very much expected that Jesus meant the Muslims to be his true followers and it is with them his Comforter who is Muhammad would live forever. I also explained to my missionary friends in brief how Muhammad who has left the world about fourteen hundred years ago, have still been living with his followers, and will continue to live until the end of the world. For my readers-both Christians and non-Christians, I shall now try to describe how this prediction of Jesus about his Comforter in John 14:16, became fulfilled through Muhammad with some valid and verifiable evidence from both Islamic and non-Islamic sources.

Islamic sources
Muhammad will abide forever through the acted examples of his life

The Quran tells the believers (3:31; 33:21; 4:65, 80; 42:52) if they really love God and hope to meet Him in their life hereafter, they should believe in His last Prophet Muhammad and follow his Sunnah (meaning the acted examples of his life that he set for them through keeping the commands of God in the Quran.) Based on that command of God, the Muslims in general, have accepted Muhammad as their role model and tried to follow his Sunnah at every walk of their life. Thus, Muhammad has remained alive with all practicing Muslims for the last fourteen hundred years through his words and deeds and will remain so until the end of the world.

Muhammad is remembered aloud ten times a day in most parts of the world

Reverend, you may feel amazed to know that Muhammad's name is remembered aloud ten times a day in most parts of the world. When a muezzin (who calls the Muslims five times a day from a local mosque to attend to their prayers), he announces some prescribed phrases twice. One of them is, "I bear witness that Muhammad is the Messenger of God."

The Muslims also make this witness for Muhammad, minimum nine times a day, and also ask God for His peace and blessing upon him minimum nineteen times a day while saying their five times obligatory prayers in their homes, mosques, or by the side of a road. Along with those obligatory prayers, they also make many optional and special prayers, and all their prayers whether obligatory, optional, or special, remain incomplete if they don't make that witness about Muhammad or ask God to bestow His peace and blessing upon him.

A moment does not pass when Muhammad's name is not remembered aloud or in silence

This remembrance of Muhammad's name aloud or in silence, becomes more intensified and incessant in both Makkah and Medina, the places of his birth and death and especially during the time of Hajj (Big Pilgrimage attended by a million once a year in commemoration of Abraham's adha or sacrifice of his son).

Most important of all, the Muslims need to invoke God for His peace and blessing upon Muhammad every time they utter, hear, read, or write his name. In fact, a moment does not pass when his name is not remembered aloud or in silence. There is also no count of how many tons of books have been written so far on various aspects of Muhammad's life only by the Muslim writers-both Arab and non-Arab to keep his name alive forever in the history of mankind.

Non-Islamic sources
Muhammad will live forever in the writing of the non-Muslim scholars

Reverend, you may believe it or not, but it is also a fact that if the Muslims stops writing about Muhammad or never wrote a word about him, he would still live forever in the writings of non-Muslim scholars especially of the Western world. To save my time and space I shall try quote some of their observation about Muhammad-the Prophet of Islam from their writing.

Let us begin first with the observation of Thomas Carlyle, a renowned Scottish philosopher, historian and a writer. In his book, *Heroes and Hero-Worship and the Heroic in History* (1840), he paid a rich tribute to Muhammad-the Messenger of God, saying:

"A man of truth and fidelity; true in what he did, in what he spake and thought...."

"A silent great soul, one of that who cannot but be earnest. He was to kindle the world, the world's Maker has ordered so."

"A false man found a religion? Why, a false man cannot build a brick house! ....It will not stand for twelve centuries, (it is fourteen centuries now) to lodge a hundred and eighty millions; (1.6 billion today-the second largest on earth) it will fall straight away......"

"The lies (western slanders) which well-meaning zeal has heaped round this man (Muhammad) are disgraceful to ourselves only."

The History of the Decline and the Fall of Roman Empire (1776) a great book written by Edward Gibbon, the famous European historian and the scholar tells us:

"The Creed of Muhammad is free from the suspicious of ambiguity and the Koran is a glorious Testimony to the unity of God."

"The Apostle of God submitted to the menial offices of the family, he kindled the fire, swept the floor, milked the ewes, and mended with his own hands his shoes and garments."

Reverend Bosworth Smith, an American Protestant Episcopal Bishop and the author of *Mohammad and Mohammadanism* (London 1874) describes:

"He (Muhammad) was a Caesar and Pope in one; but he was Pope without the Pope's pretentions, and Caesar without the legions of Caesar: without a standing army, without a bodyguard, without a palace, without a fixed revenue; if ever any man had the right to say that he ruled by the right Divine, it was Mohammad, for he had all the powers without its instruments and without its supports."

John William Draper, MD, LL.D, was a professor of chemistry and physiology and also a distinguished writer of many valuable books on the inconsistencies and the conflict in history and religion. In his book, *A History of the Intellectual Development of Europe* (London 1875), he has said:

"Four years after the death of Justinian, A.D. 569, was born in Mecca, in Arabia, the man who, of all men has exercised the greatest influence upon the human race …To be the religious head of many empires, to guide the daily life of one-third of the human race, may perhaps justify the title of a Messenger of God."

In his valuable book, *Histoire de la Turquie* (Paris, 1854), Alphonse de Lamartine, a famous French scholar wrote in appreciation of Muhammad:

….." If greatness of purpose, smallness of means and astonishing results are the three criteria of human genius, who could dare compare any great man in history with Muhammad? The most famous men created arms, laws and empires only. They founded, if anything at all, no more than material powers which often crumbled away before their eyes. This man moved not only armies, legislations, empires, peoples, dynasties, but millions of men in one-third of the then inhabited world; and more than that, he moved the altars, the gods, the religions, the ideas, the beliefs and the souls.… Philosopher, Orator, Apostle, Legislator, Conqueror of Ideas, Restorer of Rational Beliefs…the Founder of twenty terrestrial empires and of one spiritual empire, that is Muhammad. As regards all standards by which human greatness may be measured, we may all ask, is there any man greater than he?"

We may now check what George Bernard Shaw, a renowned Irish author, a playwright, and a noble prize winner, thought of Muhammad and of his religion. In his book, The Genuine Islam" Vol. 1, No 8 (1936), he said:

"If any religion had the chance of ruling over England, nay Europe within the next hundred years, it could be Islam. I have always held the religion of

Muhammad in high estimation because of its wonderful vitality. It is the only religion which appears to me to possess that assimilating capacity to the changing phases of existence which can make it appeal to every age." …..

"I have studied him-the wonderful man-and in my opinion far from being anti-Christ, he must be called the savior of humanity. I believe that if a man like him were to assume the dictatorship of the modern world, he would succeed in solving its problems in a way that would bring it the much-needed peace and happiness."

Based on the three criteria, Jules Masserman, an American Jew and a renowned psychoanalyst and a professor of Chicago University, also found Muhammad the greatest of all leaders. In his essay published in Time on July 15, 1974, he said:

"Leaders must fulfill three functions. They must provide for the well-being of those being led, provide a social organization in which people feel relatively secure, and provide them with one set of beliefs.

People like Louis Pasteur and Jonas Salk are leaders in the first sense. People like Gandhi and Confucius, Alexander, Caesar, and Hitler are leaders in the second sense. Jesus and Buddha belong in the third category alone.

Perhaps the greatest leader of all times was Muhammad, who combined all three functions. To a lesser degree, Moses did as well."

Reverend, I am going to end this part with the observation of Michael Hart, an American author and astrophysicist. In his book The 100, A Ranking of the Most Influential Persons in History (Carol Publishing Group: New York, 1989), he has reported:

"My choice of Muhammad to lead the list of the world's most influential persons may surprise some readers and may be questioned by others, but he was the only man in history who was supremely successful on both the religious and secular levels. … Muhammad founded and promulgated one of the world's great religions and became an immensely effective political leader. Today, 13 centuries after his death, his influence is still powerful and pervasive. … It is the unparalleled combination of secular and religious influence which I feel entitles Muhammad to be considered the most influential single figure in human history."

Based on those reports by the great scholars, historians, philosophers and observers of the Western world, Muslims also claim it is Muhammad-the Prophet of Islam as well as the most distinguished figure in the entire human history, whom God sent last fulfilling Jesus' prayer and prediction both.

Despite of those clear instances, if you are still in doubt and like to think, Why Muhammad, Jesus could mean someone else who has not arrived yet? The answer of your question can be sought in the meaning and implication of two Greek words 'periclytos' and paracletos'

Greek word Periclytos correspond directly to the meaning of both Muhammad and Ahmad

But before I go into that, I should first explain to you the meaning and implication of two Arabic names Muhammad and Ahmad. I already mentioned before that Ahmad is another popular name of Muhammad. Both Muhammad and Ahmad have been originated from the same root word hamdduit, himdath, or hmd in the language of Hebrew, Aramaic or Arabic which has been translated in English as "the praised one, the most laudable, altogether lovely, desire, desirable or glorified."

In that sense, if Jesus meant Muhammad or Ahmad to be his Comforter, he needed to mention his name in Aramaic as himdath, or himda, to mean someone praiseworthy, desirable, or glorified which could correspond directly to the meaning of Muhammad or Ahmad- two well-known names of the Prophet of Islam. It is interesting to note that the Greek word Periclytos corresponds directly to the meaning of hamdduit, himdath or hmd. Though the translators of the Bible from Greek to English, chose the word paracletos the meaning of which is comforter, counselor, advocate, kind, friendly, or 'one being sought for help'.

Paracletos is a corrupt reading for Periclytos

According to the observation of the modern and open-minded scholars of the Bible, the Greek word paracletos is a corrupt reading for periclytos. They think the translators of the Bible from Greek to English chose paracletos over periclytos, either intentionally or unintentionally. But instead of going into that controversy, we can also accept paracletos for Muhammad, because it also describes him perfectly well since he was well-known to his pagan kith and kin as a very generous, kind, considerate and comforting person whom they constantly sought for help, advice, or guidance long before God lauded him in the Quran as a mercy to the mankind. (21:107)

Reverend, if you still find this explanation inadequate to accept Muhammad as Jesus' Comforter or Advocate, and like to wait for someone else who has not arrived yet, in that case, I would request you to consider another prediction that God made in Haggai, 37th book of the Old Testament.

"The desire of all nations," refers to none but Muhammad -the Prophet of Islam

In the verse 7 and 9, God has declared through Prophet Haggai:

And I will shake all nations, and the desire of all nations shall come: and I will fill this house with glory, saith the Lord of the hosts....."

The glory of this latter house shall be greater than of the former, saith the Lord of the hosts: and in this place will I give peace.

Let us identify first who is the man that God has referred here as *the desire of all nations* and then we shall see how other things in the description fit with him like pieces of puzzles. The *desire* in the above quoted verses has been translated from *hamdduit* in original Hebrew, the meaning of which I already mentioned before, corresponds directly to the Greek word *periclytos* or the Arabic word *hmd*-the root word of both Muhammad and Ahmad.

this *latter house* in the verse refers to Ka'bah-the House of God at Makkah where Muhammad was born from the progeny of Ishmael-Abraham's firstborn while *the former house* refers to the House of God at Jerusalem. I think in this modern World of you tube, it is only a matter of moments to visit both the Houses of God and to judge for yourself which of the two Houses has truly surpassed the other in glory and grandeur and also in the magnitude of the devotees' submission or surrender in tears and gratitude to the same One God of Abraham, Moses, Jesus and Muhammad.

Last of all, remains *peace* and it has been translated into English from the Hebrew word *shalom*, the meaning of which is identical with Arabic root word *slm* from where *salaam or the name of Islam*-the world-shaking religion of God was originated and given to Muhammad at Makkah, nearly six hundred years after Jesus' ascent to heaven.

Jesus' Testifier is undoubtedly Muhammad-the last and the final Prophet of God

Reverend, you may know it or not, but according to the projected data of the Pew Report, if Islam-the latest and the fastest growing religion of the world maintains its current rate of growth undisturbed, the number of its adherents which is now 1.6 billion, will reach to 1.76 by 2050 and by the end of the century it will be the largest on this planet, when one of three persons will be a Muslim. Taking all those observation and evidence in consideration, we have no doubt in mind that Jesus' Comforter, Advocate, or Testifier is no one else but Muhammad-the last and the final Prophet of God. In that case, the possibility of Muhammad's living forever with his followers is bound to rocket up, proving Jesus' prediction about his Comforter in John 14:16, to be true to the letter.

In fact, we have been claiming Muhammad as Jesus' Comforter or Advocate unopposed for the last fourteen hundred years, since God sent him along with Quran testifying of Jesus' true status and mission and clearing his name from all the myths, misconceptions and the false doctrines that his followers began cherishing in his name as the indispensable parts of their faith, after he left. I intend to address those issues one by one in the rest of my letters where I shall try to justify my claim by Jesus' own statements in the Gospel, and also by the testimony of the Quran that God has sent through His last Prophet Muhammad.

"O Jesus! I will take you and raise you to Myself and clear you [of the falsehood] from those who blasphemy.

I will make those superior who follow you to those who reject faith until the Day of Resurrection. Then you all return to Me and I will judge between you in the matters wherein you differ."
(Quran 3:55)

Letter 6

True Meaning and Implication of the Name "Christ" and "Word"

To the Jews who had believed him, Jesus said, "If you hold to my teaching, you are really my disciples. Then you will know the truth, and the truth will set you free."

—John 8:31–32

Reverend,

In my last letter, I mentioned that Muhammad was sent after Jesus as his testifier fulfilling his prediction and prayer both and also making him free from the blaspheme of all the myths, misconceptions and invented doctrines that his followers began cherishing in his name as the integral parts of their faith, after he left. In this letter, I intend to discuss some of Jesus' popular names or titles that his followers took to be completely mystic, mysterious, or "Divine" in nature, which finally led them to worship him as God, or God Incarnate. Let us begin with his name "Christ."

Some of my missionary friends told me Jesus was the only "Begotten" of God and he remained with Him as an inseparable part before the beginning of the creation. They also believe the name "Christ" was kept hidden by God Himself for His only begotten. So, when Jesus was born without a father and was called "Christ," they took him for God Incarnate meaning God appeared Himself in flesh through His only begotten Jesus. I found this description close to the Paganism and completely contradictory to the pure and pristine monotheism in the teaching of all the prophets of God including Jesus himself.

After I studied the Bible, the Quran, and other authentic books on Comparative Religion, I understood the true meaning and the implication of the name "Christ" was completely different from what they believed to be true in good faith. Let me explain it with evidence and instances in support of that.

Both "Christ" and "Messiah" are synonymous

The word "Christ" comes from the Greek word Christos, meaning anointed or appointed. And Christos was translated into Greek from the Hebrew word mashiyach, which also means to anoint, to rub, or to appoint. In Arabic, it is called masih, meaning simply a chosen, promised or a designated messenger of God.

There is a long-rooted tradition among the Jews related to their religious faith and practices. They used to anoint their prophets, priests, or kings ceremonially before they held their position, rank, or authority. Accordingly, the person who was anointed or appointed in this way was also called Messiah or Christ by their people. In that sense, both "Christ" and "Messiah" are synonymous.

In the following instances of the Bible, we shall try to know how the procedure of getting someone anointed took place in the Jewish community.

(Leviticus 8:10) *And Moses took the anointing oil, and anointed the tabernacle and all that was therein, and sanctioned them.*

(1 Samuel 16:13) *Then Samuel took the horn of oil, and anointed him [David] in the midst of his brethren.*

(2 Samuel 22:51) *He gives his king great victories; he shows unfailing kindness to his anointed, to David and to his descendants forever.*

(Isaiah 45:1) *Thus saith the Lord to his anointed, to Cyrus, whose right hand I have holden ...*

The oppressed people used to believe God would send His Messiah for their relief

According to the description of the Judeo-Christian and Islamic tradition, we came to know the oppressed, the deprived and the God-fearing people used to wait eagerly for the arrival of a promised messenger of God whom they called Messiah or Christ. They expected him to come and deliver them from the hands of their oppressors. They knew about his arrival through the prophecies of other prophets who were sent before them. It was the only reason Pharaoh-the tyrant king of Egypt who subjugated the descendants of Israel as his slaves, began to kill their sons when he heard about the arrival of a Messiah from them as their savior. Long after the arrival and departure of Moses, the Roman authority also began to kill the sons of the Israelite who were then expecting the Christ or the Messiah to come and to deliver them from their slavery or subjugation.

Similarly, many Jews began to settle in Medina or the city of the Prophet, long before Muhammad-the Prophet of Islam arrived and migrated there from his hometown Makkah to save his life and his religion from the persecution of his own Pagan kith and kin. The Jews knew about his arrival from their holy scripture and in the prophecies of Moses and other prophets of God. Based on that religious and historical evidence, we may rightly claim both "Christ and "Messiah" are synonymous. The Jews used to call the promised messenger of God as the Messiah or the Christ. I have quoted below some statements from both Bible and Quran to justify my claim.

(Duet 18:18) *I will raise them up a prophet from among their brethren, like unto thee, and will put my words in his mouth; and he shall speak unto them all that I shall command him.*

(John 4:25–26) *The woman said, "I know that Messiah, called Christ, is coming. When he comes, he will explain everything to us." Then Jesus declared, "I, the one speaking to you-I am he."*

(John10:23–24) *And Jesus walked in the temple in Solomon's porch. Then came the Jews round about him, and said unto him, "How long dost thou make us to doubt? If thou be the Christ, tell us plainly."*

(Quran 3:45) *.. the angels said, "O Mary! Verily, Allah gives you the glad tidings of a Word from Him: his name will be Christ Jesus, son of Mary.*

Thus, the scriptures of God have made it clear to us there is no hidden mystery in the name of Christ. It is but a title of Jesus whom God chose to send as one of His unique and special messengers for the guidance of his own people-the misguided Jews (Matthew 15:24).

Other prophets also had God-given names or titles

In this connection, I would like to point out that it was not Jesus alone, many other chosen messengers of God also received their names and titles from God Himself. Following instances from both Bible and Quran have been cited for your consideration.

(Genesis 16:11) *And the angel of the Lord said unto her [Hagar], Behold, thou art with child, and shalt bear a son, and shall call his name Ishmael, because the Lord hath heard thy affliction.*

(Genesis 17:19) *And God said, Sarah thy wife [by this time God had changed Abram's name to Abraham and his wife Sarai's, name to Sarah] shall bear thee a son indeed; ; and thou shalt call his name Isaac. ... ...*

(Genesis 35:10) *And God said unto him, Thy name is Jacob: thy name shall not be called any more Jacob, but Israel shall be thy name: and he called his name Israel.*

(Quran 4:125) *Who can be better in religion than one who submits his whole self to Allah, does good and follows the way of Abraham-the Hanif. For Allah did take Abraham as His Khalil [friend].*

The meaning of Hanif in Arabic refers to a person who is upright by nature and the upholder of pure and pristine monotheism-the eternal truth in the guidance of God. Khalil means friend and because of that Abraham is known and respected among the Muslims as Khalilullah, meaning Friend of Allah.

(Quran 4:164) *And messengers We have mentioned to you before, and messengers We have not mentioned to you, and to Moses Allah spoke directly.*

Moses is also known and respected in the Muslim world as Kalimullah, meaning to whom God spoke directly. This part was translated in English from the Arabic version 'wa kallamallaahu Muusaa takliimaa."

Jesus is known to the Muslims by three significant names

According to the description of both Quran and the authentic Hadith, Jesus was called Masih Jesus or the Christ Jesus meaning a chosen messenger of God. The Quran says:

(3:45) *... the angels said, "O Mary! Verily, Allah gives you the glad tidings of a Word from Him: his name will be Messiah/Christ Jesus, son of Mary.*

As Mary conceived Jesus by God's commanding word "Be," he is also called "Kalimatullah" meaning the Word of God. The Quran also confirms it in the following verse where Allah says to Zachariah:

(3:39) *Allah gives you [Zachariah] glad tidings of Yahya [John the Baptist] confirming the Word from Allah [meaning the creation of Jesus by His commanding word "Be"]*

(3:47) She [Mary] said: *'O my Lord! How shall I have a son when no man has ever touched me?'* He said: *'Even so. God creates what He wills; when He decides to do anything, He only says to it, 'Be' and it is!*

Jesus is also called Ruhullah, meaning the Spirit of God.

The Quran says: *And We blessed the woman (Mary), who guarded her chastity, We breathed into her of Our Spirit and We made her and her son a sign for the whole world.* (21:91)

Similarly, Muhammad- the last and the final Prophet of God, is called Nabial Ummi, meaning the Unlettered Prophet; Khataman nabiun, meaning the Seal of the Prophets, and as Rahmatal- lil-aalamiin, meaning a blessing for the whole world. He is called so by his people from the description of the following verses in the Quran.

(7:157) *Those who follow the Apostle—the unlettered prophet [Muhammad] whom they find mentioned in the Torah and the Gospel; for he commands them what is just and forbids them what is evil.*

(33:40) *Muhammad is not the father of any of your men. He is the Apostle of Allah and the Seal of the Prophets.*

(21:107) *We have sent you (Muhammad) not, but as a mercy to the mankind.*

According to the description of the Quran (3:84) Muslims do not make any distinction or difference among the Prophets of God since all of them were sent to accomplish the same mission which is to proclaim the worship of One True Eternal God among their people. Muslims also believe, God chose those special names and titles for Jesus and others for a reason. It is to specify them from one another by some of their special acts, traits, or qualities, or by some extraordinary circumstances or condition of their life. To call people with other names or titles besides their real name, is also a common practice found everywhere in the world. The only difference is God-given names or titles for His chosen persons, is plain, simple, unbiased, dignified and are meant to last forever.

Frankly speaking, we should consider the name Christ most appropriate and significant for Jesus, because he was not given any special name or title like any of his predecessors or his successor-Muhammad. Jesus was called

Christ the meaning of which is simply a chosen or a designated Messenger of God. We may now rightly assume that, God Who encompasses everything in His knowledge and vision, knew perfectly well that a day would come after Jesus, when his followers would begin to worship him as God by forgetting his true status, role or mission of a Prophet whom He sent for the guidance of his own people-the misguided Jews. (Matthew 15:24)

So, by the name "Christ," God made it clear to all that though He made Jesus unique and special in many ways, he was but one of His messengers who was assigned to guide the people to His path as did all his predecessors before him.

An unexpected visitor arrives in the middle of my writing

Reverend, something quite unexpected happened when I was in the middle of my writing. I was visited by a missionary lady with a copy of Bible in her hand. I felt myself quite excited to think that I could share with her certain things about Jesus, especially at that moment when I was writing about the mystery of his name and title in the light of both Bible and Quran.

She was probably in her mid-forties, tall, slim, and light-skinned. She also looked very modest and dignified in her long-sleeve white blouse and long black skirt that matched perfectly with her black cap and black shoes. I took a moment to appreciate a perfect blend of beauty and brightness standing right before me, after I opened the door at the ring of the bell.

While walking to the living room through a short hallway, she, let's call her Mrs. Martha Miller, told me she was a teacher of science in the local high school and a volunteer worker for the local Church of the Trinity. I also told her a few things about me. She looked happy when I said that I was also a teacher like her before I came to America. She seemed to be a bit reserved when I told her I was a Muslim. But she could not hide her delight when I mentioned to her about my special love and respect for Jesus.

We took our seat in the living room couches face to face with a coffee table in between, the top of which was loaded with my lap, two books on the meaning of the Quran in both English and in my mother tongue Bengali; two copies of the Bible in the version of KJV and NIV; several books on Islam and Christianity along with notepads, pencil-holders, a bottle of water, a bowl of mixed nuts and also a box of soft tissue. Mrs. Miller was kind enough to ignore the mess. She put her own Bible on the side table beside her and then exclaimed happily, "Oh, my God, do you read Bible?"

"Yes Madam." Then I added humbly, "I have been reading it seriously for more than a year."

"But as far as I know your Holy Book is Quran that Muhammad claimed to receive from God, Right?"

"Right, but along with the Quran a Muslim is also required to believe in all the scriptures of God and in all His messengers who were sent before Muhammad."

"It is interesting, because I know many Muslims who avoid us if they find us with a Bible."

"Maybe, they are too busy to waste their time on something which they already know."

"You mean they also read the Bible as they read the Quran?"

"No, I mean," I tried to clarify, "They know about Jesus, Moses, Abraham and other prominent prophets of the Bible from the study of the Quran. But my case is different," I added in a hurry, "I read the Bible, because I'm writing about Jesus as I found him in both Quran and the Gospel."

"Really! It's so wonderful!" Mrs. Miller exclaimed in delightful surprise. "Thanks! Besides that, I am very fond of religion and I hardly get tired to listen to it or to talk about it. It is the only reason I welcome all my Christian Missionary friends who often come to me to talk about Jesus. In fact, when I saw you first," I admitted to her happily, "I felt you were God-sent, because I found a verse in the Gospel a little complicated and I instantly thought you might help me to understand it."

"May I please know which verse?" She asked sweetly while picking up her Bible from the side table.

"It is the first verse in the first chapter of John. Do you want me to read?" I picked up the copy of the KJV and I became happy to see she also had the same version.

"Just give me a second," she said, while turning over the pages of her

Bible. Then she stopped, saying, "Yes, here it is. You may now read."

In the beginning was the Word, and the Word was with God, and the Word was God.

It was a short verse, but I tried to read it slowly and as correctly as possible with my unavoidable foreign accent. *In the beginning was the Word, and the Word was with God, and the Word was God.* (John 1:1)

After I finished reading, I said to her politely, "Some of my missionary friends told me the 'Word' in the verse refers to Jesus and God both. But I feel confused because the verse didn't mention anything like that. So, I don't understand how the 'Word' in the verse refers to Jesus and God both."

"I understand your confusion," Said Mrs. Miller gracefully. "But you need to remember the verses of the Bible are complementary to one another. It means to understand the meaning of the verse 1, you also have to read the verse 14 below it." I saw Mrs. Miller to put her index finger on verse 14, which I read for no less than twenty times since I started writing about Jesus' true status from the narration of both Bible and Quran.

I tried to listen to her minutely when she said, "Okay, let me read the verse and explain to you." And she began to read in her soft, sweet, and well-modulated voice. *And the Word was made flesh, and dwelt among us, (and we beheld his glory, the glory of as of the only begotten of the Father,) full of grace and truth. (John 1:14)*

After she finished reading, she looked up at me and then began to explain it as confidently as possible, "I think now you can see the connection, because this verse has mentioned clearly the 'Word,' referring to God in verse 1, was made flesh. It tells us God appeared Himself in the physical form of His only Son Jesus, and then dwelled among the people, with full of grace and truth. I hope, now it is clear to you, right?" She sounded to me very cool and confident.

"Please excuse me for my shortcomings and I." I said to her with a bit hesitation. "But there are some elements," I tried to point out, "in the verses 1 and 14 that I still find confusing. For example, you said the 'Word' in both the verses refers to God and Jesus equally. But I don't see how, because the 'Word' didn't come into existence by itself. It was made flesh in the physical form of Jesus and then it was sent to earth to dwell among the people, Right?"

"Yes, it is what the verse said, so where is your confusion?"

"I'm confused because I still don't understand how the Maker and being made or the Sender and being sent can be considered as one and the same?"

"I think you've missed the link completely," said Mrs. Miller very politely. "It is God Himself who made Him appear in the form of Jesus. In that case, the question of the Maker and being made does not arise at all."

Do you want me to believe that it was God Who begot Himself in the womb of Virgin Mary and then manifested Himself on earth through Jesus! But I kept my question to myself and said to her instead,

"Sorry, I still have some confusion. The verse 14 has mentioned beholding of his glory, the glory as of the only begotten of the Father in parenthesis. Do you have any idea why such an important statement on God's appearance through His only begotten Jesus has been put in the parenthesis?"

"Frankly speaking," Mrs. Miller said being patient and polite, "This type of question does not bother a true Christian, because whatever their Bible says, within the parenthesis or without it, they believe it as the word of God without any question or confusion."

Jesus was also mentioned in the Quran as the "Word of God."

After this straightforward answer, I thought I should better stop mentioning anything to her from the Gospel. I should rather, tell her what the Quran has said about Jesus as the "Word of God". May be, she would find my explanation more reasonable than what she just explained to me. So, I supported her saying, "Sure. A true believer in God should take His words in the scripture seriously. I think you will be happy to know that our Holy Book Quran also describes Jesus as the "Word of God".

"Really?" She sounded happy and relaxed.

"Yes, and we also don't mind to believe Jesus remained with God as His Word from the beginning."

"Then why can't you accept him being equal to God?"

"We can't, because we believe it is not only Jesus, everything in the creation of God has remained with God in His ultimate plan from the beginning which comes into existence by His direct command or according to His Preset timetable. There are many verses in the Quran where we have been told that whenever God wants to do anything, He just says to it, 'Be,' and it is.

"Same thing happened when God wanted Virgin Mary to conceive her son Jesus. He just commanded, "Be," and she conceived. Let me read to you some verses of the Quran from my lap in support of that."

My lap was already in sleep, so it did not take me long to reach my file by the name Jesus. I read to her following three verses of the Quran after I opened my file.

(3:47) *She [Mary] said: 'O my Lord! How shall I have a son when no man has ever touched me?' He said: 'Even so. God creates what He wills; when He decides to do anything, He only says to it, 'Be' and it is!*

(3:39)....*Allah gives you [Zachariah] glad tidings of Yahya [John the Baptist] confirming the Word from Allah [meaning the creation of Jesus by His commanding word 'Be'].*

(3:59) *Verily, the likeness of Jesus before Allah is as the likeness of Adam. He created him (Adam) from dust, then He said to him: "Be" and he was.*

After I finished reading, I looked up at Mrs. Miller and said, "I hope now you know why the Muslims have no problem to accept Jesus as the 'Word' of God, but have problem to accept him as God, God Incarnate or being equal to God."

Mrs. Miller remained silent.

The Bible says, "Let there be," while the Quran says, "Be"

Luckily, by this time I finished reading most of the books of the Bible, beginning from Genesis-the First Book of Moses, and I remembered very well how the creation of God came into existence. So, I said to her reminding, "Mrs. Miller, you certainly have read the first Book of the Old Testament and remember how God created light and other things of His creations, Right?"

Mrs. Miller looked apprehensive and said, "Yes I do."

"Then, you also remember what God did when He wanted to create light. He just said, "Let there be light," and there was light. He commanded the same before His other creations. Doesn't it tell us," I asked her politely, "That God used more or less the same commanding word to bring things into existence, as it is mentioned in the Quran?"

After a moment of silence, I said to her again, "So, I don't understand how the Commander and His commanding word "Let there be" or a simple "Be" can be considered as one and the same?"

"May I please know, Mrs. Miller asked me again very politely, "If everything in the world was with God from the beginning and then came to existence by His Commanding Word "Be," why then Jesus alone was called the "Word of God?"

"Good question. I also pondered over the matter for quite some time.

Then I thought Jesus was called so because God wanted his followers to know and remember how his virgin mother conceived him by His commanding word "Be" or "Let there be" so that they could never mistake him for God or...."

"Sorry to interrupt you," Mrs. Miller said looking at her wristwatch, "I have to leave now to attend a seminar in my church."

"Sure. But I thank you very much because you are a very good listener."

"Don't mention it, please. I really had no idea the Quran has said so much about Jesus."

"Yes. I think, the more we know about each other's faith, the better we know who we are and what God wanted us to do." I said honestly while walking to the door with her.

"You are right. We can share a lot through talking to each other." Then she surprised me saying with a charming smile, "I'll come again soon, I promise."

"Thanks. I'll be waiting for you."

We shook our hands warmly and she left gracefully after I opened the door and held it for her.

Interpretation of the "Word" as found in the Modern Versions of the Bible.

Reverend, a few weeks after Mrs. Miller left, I had a chance to read the interpretation of the "Word" in John 1.1 in some Modern Versions of the Bible. I like to share that with you and with my other readers-both Christians and non-Christians.

Modern scholars and the interpreters of the Bible tell us that in the original Greek manuscript, the Word was used to mean divine or god, and it was never used to mean Divine or God. Accordingly, the New World Translation of the Bible has translated John 1:1 as follows:

In the beginning was the Word and the Word was with God, and the Word was divine.

The Dictionary of the Bible by John McKenzie translates John 1:1 as follows: *The word was with God [the Father] and the word was a divine being.*

By their interpretation, they have unknowingly confirmed those verses of the Quran where Jesus was addressed as the "word" of God and was described as being noble, chaste, righteous, and close to God whom He sent as His Messenger for the guidance of his own people. (3:39, 3:45-51).

On Jesus' Incarnation: A report from Grolier's Encyclopedia

Reverend, I think, it will not be irrelevant, if I mention here another essential element of your faith related to Jesus' incarnation, meaning God manifested Himself in flesh through Jesus. I would like to draw your attention to the following statement, which I have quoted below from the Grolier's Encyclopedia, for your kind perusal.

"Incarnation denotes the embodiment of a deity in human form. The idea occurs frequently in mythology. In ancient times, certain people, especially kings and priests, were often believed to be divinities. In Hinduism, Vishnu is believed to have nine incarnations, or Avatars. For Christians, the incarnation is a central dogma referring to the belief that the eternal son of God, the second person of the Trinity, became man in the person of Jesus Christ. The incarnation was defined as a doctrine only after long struggles by early Church Council. The Council of Nicaea (325 CE) defined the deity of Christ against Aryanism; the Council of Constantinople (381 CE) defined the full humanity of the incarnate Christ against Apollinarianism; the Council of Ephesus (431 CE) defined the unity of Christ's person against Nestorianism; and the council of Chalcedon (451 CE) defined the two natures of Christ, divine and human, against Eutyches."

The statement in Grolier's Encyclopedia makes it clear to all how Jesus, the son of Mary, was gradually turned into a human God or became an object of worship by his followers, after he left.

Transgression was made in the Book of God to validate Jesus' Incarnation

The only verse quoted so far to validate the doctrine of incarnation was also proved to be a forgery about six centuries after Jesus' ascent to heaven. It is also interesting to note that after its official injunction into the Christian faith, the Council of Churches needed biblical evidence to serve their purpose. Accordingly, they made a subtle change in 1Timothy 3:16. Please have a look how this verse was read before and after the incarnation was made an essential doctrine of the Christian faith.

1 Timothy 3:16, (as read before the sixth-century amendment):

And without ceremony great is the mystery of godliness: which was manifest in the flesh, justified in the Spirit, seen of angels, preached unto the gentiles, believed on in the world, received up into glory.

1 Timothy 3:16, *(as read after the sixth-century amendment):*

And without controversy great is the mystery of godliness: God was manifest in the flesh, justified in the Spirit, seen of angels, preached unto the Gentiles, believed on in the world, received up into glory.

Reverend, hope, it is now clear to you how the transgression was made to validate Jesus' incarnation by changing godliness to God. For the truth-seeking people, it is a matter of great relief that the modern and the open-minded scholars of the Bible have been trying hard to detect those unauthorized addition, or elimination in the Book of God and to bring the truth to the knowledge of the public.

> He [Jesus] was no more than a servant: We granted Our favor to him and made him an example to the Children of Israel.
> (Quran 43:59).

Letter 7

Jesus Was Declared a Prophet of God in both Gospel and Quran

And the multitude said, this is Jesus the Prophet of Nazareth of Galileeee.

- Matthew 21:11

Reverend,

The Quran which God revealed upon His last Prophet Muhammad about fourteen hundred years ago, reminds us repeatedly that Jesus was a mighty Messenger of God from the House of Israel, and he was sent to establish the worship of One True God among his own people and to guide them to His path as did all his predecessors before him. But most of the Christians-both elite and illiterate like to believe Muhammad is a false prophet and so is the Quran that he claimed to receive from God as His last and final guidebook for all of mankind. It is only for them I have tried to quote those statements from the Gospel as well as from the Quran where Jesus' role and mission as a Prophet of God has been made distinctly clear.

The Gospel tells us Jesus was a Prophet of God

(Matthew 15:24) *But he [Jesus] answered and said, I am not sent but unto the lost sheep of the house of Israel.*

(Matthew 21:11) *And the multitude said, This is Jesus the prophet of Nazareth of Galilee.*

(Mark 6:4) *But Jesus said unto them, a prophet [referring to him when his own people offended him by their disrespectful attitude towards him] is not without honor but in his own country, and among his own kin, and in his own house.*

(Luke 4:43) *And he [Jesus] said unto them, I must preach the kingdom of God to other cities also: for therefore am I sent.*

(Luke 24:19) *And he [Jesus] said unto them, What things? And they said unto him, Concerning Jesus of Nazareth, which was a prophet mighty in deed and word before God and all the people.*

(John 4:19, 25-26) *"Sir,"* The woman said, *"I can see that you are a prophet. The woman said, I know that Messiah called Christ is coming. When he comes, he will explain everything to us."*

Then Jesus declared, "I, the one speaking to you-I am he."

(John 6:14) *After the people saw the sign Jesus performed, they began to say, "Surely, this is the Prophet who is to come into the world."*

(John 7:40) *On hearing his words, some of the people said, "Surely, this man is the Prophet."*

(Acts 2:22) *"Ye men of Israel, hear these words; Jesus of Nazareth-a man approved of God among you by miracles and wonders and signs, which God did by him in the midst of you, as ye yourselves also know."*

The message of the above-quoted verses is explicitly clear. Jesus knew himself he was a Prophet of God and people of his time knew that, too. If Jesus knew he were God or His equal, as you claim, why did he introduce himself falsely as the Prophet of God or allow his people to remain in the dark about his true identity or status? The fact is, Jesus had nothing to hide about him, so he told them honestly who he really was and why he was sent for.

Jesus made his role and mission clear to his people

Jesus is known to dwell with them a short span of life calling and teaching them constantly and consistently to worship none but One God and to strive for their eternal life through keeping His commands, as did all his predecessors before him.

(Mark 12:29–30) *And Jesus answered him [a Jewish scribe], The first of all the commandments is, Hear, O Israel, the LORD our GOD is ONE LORD: And thou shalt love the LORD thy GOD with all thy heart, and with all thy soul, and with all thy mind and with all thy strength: this is the first commandment.*

(Matthew 4:10) *In reply to all the lucrative offers of the Satan (Matthew 4:8-9), Jesus said to him in disgust, "Get thee hence, Satan for it is written, THOU SHALT WORSHIP THE LORD THY GOD, AND HIM ONLY SHALT THOU SERVE."*

(Matthew 19:16–17) *And behold, one came and said unto him [to Jesus], Good Master, what good thing shall I do, that I may have eternal life?*

And he said unto him, Why callest thou me good? There is none good but one, that is, God: but if thou wilt enter into life, keep the commandments.

By this advice to the young man, Jesus made it absolutely clear that it were none but God Who alone is all perfect, and man should strive for the eternal life through keeping His commands meaning the Laws of the Torah that Moses received from God.

(Matthew 5:17) Do not think that I have come to abolish the Law or the prophets; I have not come to abolish them but to fulfill them.

(Luke 4:43) And he said unto them, I must preach the kingdom of God to other cities also: for therefore am I sent.

(John 9:4) I must work the works of him that sent me.

(John 12:44) Jesus cried and said, He that believeth on me, believeth not on me, but on him that sent me.

(John 17:3) Now this is eternal life: that they know you, the only true God, and Jesus Christ, whom you have sent.

In those statements that I quoted above from different parts of the Gospel, Jesus also admitted himself clearly who sent him and why he was sent for.

Jesus was a special Messenger of God: Instances from the Quran

Reverend, you may know it or not, but the Quran also testifies through Muhammad Jesus was a unique and a special Messenger of God from the House of Israel and he was sent for the guidance of his own people. I have quoted below some verses from the Quran where you will find Jesus' status, role or mission is in complete harmony with the statements in the Gospel-the Book you believe yourself as a true account of Jesus' own words and deeds.

(3:39) While he [Zakariya] was standing in a prayer in the chamber, the angel called upon him [saying]: Allah gives you the good news of Yahya [John, the Baptist], witnessing the truth of a Word [meaning Jesus] from Allah who will be noble, chaste and a Prophet from among the righteous.

(3:42, 48-49) Behold! The angels said: "O Mary! Allah has chosen you and purified you, above the women of all nations. ... Allah will teach your son the Book, the Wisdom, the Torah, and the Gospel, and will make him a Messenger to the children of Israel ...

(4:171) O people of the Book [meaning the Christians]! Do not exceed the

limits in your religion, nor say of Allah anything but the truth. The Messiah Jesus, the son of Mary was no more than a Messenger of God.

The Quran also tells us Jesus testified himself as a Prophet of God from his cradle in response to peoples' slander against Mary, his virgin mother.

(19:29–30) *Then she [Mary] pointed to him [her son in the cradle]. They said: How can we talk to one who is a child in the cradle? He [Jesus] said, I am indeed a servant of God; He has given me revelation and made me a Prophet.*

(3:50-51) *[Jesus said to his people] I am appointed to confirm that which is before me from the Torah and to make lawful to you some of the things forbidden to you. Now I have brought the signs from your Lord, therefore fear God, and obey me. In fact, Allah is my Lord as well as your Lord, therefore, Worship Him; this is the right Way.*

The Quran also reminds us clearly Jesus was sent for the guidance of his people following the footsteps of all his predecessors. God says in the Quran:

We gave Moses the Book and followed him with a succession of Apostles: We gave Jesus, the son of Mary clear Signs and strengthened him with the Holy Spirit. (2:87)

Then in the footsteps of those Prophets, We sent Jesus the son of Mary confirming whatever remained intact from the Torah in his time, and gave him the Gospel wherein was guidance and light, corroborating what was revealed in the Torah; a guidance and an abomination to those who fear God. (5:46)

When Jesus came with clear signs, he said: Now I have come to you with wisdom and to make clear to you some of those issues about which you dispute; therefore fear Allah and obey me. (43:63)

Based on those clear statements of the Quran that God revealed to His last Prophet Muhammad about fourteen hundred years ago, all his followers have accepted, loved, and respected Mary as a chaste, truthful and an illustrious woman of the world, and her son Jesus as a noble, righteous and a chosen Messenger of God without knowing anything of what the Gospel has really said about him or about his mother.

Jesus was a self-surrendered slave or servant of God

According to the description of both Bible and Quran, we also have learnt that all the messengers of God including Jesus and Muhammad, surrendered to Him completely as His slaves or servants. Rightly so, because God has sent them to accomplish His mission which is to establish His worship among their people and to guide them to His Path so that they could return to Him-their ultimate Refuge safely, and without being confused or misled. To fulfill this mission, they left nothing unsaid or undone of what God commanded them to do for the guidance of their people. It is for their total submission or surrender to God, they were addressed in the Quran as *Ibaadinaal Mursaleen* (in Arabic) meaning our slaves, the messengers. I have quoted below some verses from both parts of the Bible as well as from the Quran, to justify my point.

Instances from the Old Testament

(Exodus 32:13) *Remember your servants Abraham, Isaac, and Israel, to whom you swore by your own self: I will make your descendants as numerous as the stars in the sky and I will multiply your seed as the stars of heaven...*

(Joshua 1:1) *After the death of Moses the servant of the LORD, the LORD said to Joshua son of Nun,......*

(2 Samuel 7:20) *What more can David say to you? For you know your servant, Sovereign LORD.*

(Job 2:3) *Then the LORD said to Satan, "Have you considered my servant Job? There is no one on earth like him; he is blameless and upright, a man who fears God and shuns evil.*

(Isaiah 44:1) *Yet now hear, O Jacob my servant; and Israel, whom I have chosen.*

(Daniel 9:17) *Now therefore, O our God, hear the prayer of thy servant [Daniel], and his supplications, and cause thy face to shine upon thy sanctuary that is desolate, for the Lord's sake.*

Instances from the New Testament

(John 13:16) *Very truly I tell you, no servant* [Jesus compares himself to a servant] *is greater than his master, nor is a messenger greater than the one who sent him.*

(Acts 3:13) *The God of Abraham, Isaac and Jacob, the God of our fathers, has glorified his servant Jesus.*

(Acts 3:26) *Unto you first God, having raised his Son Jesus, sent him to bless you, in turning away every one of you from his iniquities.*

At this point, it is interesting note that the King James Version has used 'Son' to describe Jesus in both the statements of the Acts while the NIV has used servant. I shall try to explain this confusion about the 'son' and the 'servant' in the next chapter while describing Jesus' status as the Son of God and the Son of man.

Instances from the Quran

The following passages of the Quran tell us about some of the messengers of God who obtained His special favors and mercies for their complete submission and surrender to Him.

(27:15) *We gave [in the past] knowledge to David and Solomon: and they both said: Praise be to Allah Who has favored us above many of His servants who believe!*

(37:171–173) *We have already promised Our servants whom We sent as Our Messengers that they would certainly be helped, and that our forces (the true believers and the righteous) will surely be victorious.*

(43:59) *He [Jesus] was no more than a servant. We granted Our favor to him, and We made him an example to the children of Israel.*

(4:172) *The Messiah [Jesus] will never be proud to reject to be a slave to God, nor the angels who are nearest [to God].*

(17:1) *Glory to Allah Who did take His servant [Muhammad] for journey by night from the Sacred Mosque of Mecca to the Farthest Mosque [in Jerusalem.]*

Jesus did everything by the command of God and for the sake of His Pleasure

Reverend, while reading the Gospel, you must have come across many verses where Jesus admitted himself clearly that he did not say or do anything on his own accord. Rather, he did everything by the command of God and for the sake of His Pleasure.

(John 5:30) *I can of mine own self do nothing: as I hear, I judge: and my judgment is just; because I seek not mine own will, but the will of the Father which hath sent me.*

(John 12:49) *For I have not spoken of myself; but the Father which sent me, he gave me a commandment, what I should say, and what I should speak.*

(John 8:29) *And he [God] that sent me is with me: the Father hath not left me alone; for I do always those things that please him.*

I think no explanation is required to understand the message of those verses that I quoted above. Who but the most devoted and dedicated servant of God would try to perform his assigned job so humbly and wholeheartedly as Jesus claimed to do?

Opinion of the Anglican Bishops about Jesus' true status: Points to ponder

On June 25, 1984, the London Daily News ran an article titled "Shock Survey of Anglican Bishops," which described a survey report regarding Jesus' true status. A poll, conducted by the religious television show Credo, showed that more than half of the Anglican Bishops in England said Christians were not obliged to believe that Jesus Christ was God. The article further stated that nineteen of the thirty-one Bishops agreed that "it is sufficient to regard Jesus as God's supreme agent."

God's "supreme agent" refer to none but the chosen or the designated messengers of God whom He sent from time to time for the guidance of their people. The Anglican Bishops' comment about Jesus in the survey report in 1984 is similar, to what God said about him in the Quran nearly six hundred years after his ascent to heaven.

> *Christ, the son of Mary, was no more than a messenger. Many messengers had already passed away before him. His mother was a truthful woman; they both ate earthly food like other human beings. See how the revelations are made clear to them to know the reality; yet see how they ignore the truth."*
> *Holy Quran (5:75)*

Letter 8

Jesus as the Son of God and as the Son of Man

(To Muhammad) Say: He is God, The One and Only; God, the Self-Sufficient. He begets not, Nor He is begotten; and there is none equal or comparable to Him.

—Holy Quran 112:1–4

Reverend,

In this letter, I intend to discuss whether Jesus was truly the "only begotten and beloved son of God," as his devoted followers claim about him, or he was the "son of man," meaning a man of flesh and blood whom God sent as His messenger for the guidance of his own people-the misguided Jews. I shall of course discuss the matter upon the evidence of our Holy Scriptures-the Bible and the Quran both.

Why Jesus called God his Father and him His Son?

No Muslim believes Jesus called God his Father and him as the son of God to mean he was really begotten by God as a human father begets his children, and therefore the question of taking Jesus and his Father in the heaven being one and the same, does not arise to them at all. They consider this Father-Son relationship in between God and Jesus completely from a different perspective. They believe Jesus called God his Father to show his intense love and longing for Him and to be close with Him through obeying His commands that He bestowed upon him as His Messenger. It is a kind of feeling that a concerned, caring, loyal, obedient and a grateful son always nourishes in his heart to please his most loving, compassionate, competent, and adorable father. Jesus also knew that his virgin mother conceived him by the command of God, and because of that he might have felt very much close or connected with Him when he called God His Father and him as His son.

The status of God is the highest of all

Reverend, I do not think I need any assumed excuses or explanations to make you or others believe the status of God is the highest of all and no one can attain it by any means. We also have Jesus' own statement in the Gospel to verify whether by calling God as his Father and him as His son, he ever meant himself being equal to God by he had the same status, wisdom, authority, knowledge, and power like Him. We may now examine the meaning and implication of the following statements of Jesus that he made to his disciples about his amazing acts of miracles.

(John 5:19–20) *Jesus gave them this answer: "Very truly I tell you, the Son can do nothing by himself; he can do only what he sees his Father doing, because whatever the Father does the son also does. For the Father loves the Son and shows him all he does. Yes, and he will show him even greater works than these, so that you will be amazed.*

(John 11:4) *When Jesus heard that, he said, "This sickness will not end in death. No, it is for God's glory so that God's Son may be glorified through it."*

In those verses, we find Jesus to admit to his people openly that the Son could do nothing by himself. Whatever astonishing or amazing acts he performed to them so far, he did them being inspired by his Father in heaven Who is the source of all power and knowledge and the Disposer of all affairs in the entire heavens and earth. Jesus also told his disciples that God would glorify him more to make his status high before them. He told them so because as an inspired Messenger of God, he knew in advance that God would bring his dead friend Lazarus back to life through him. People of his community already knew Lazarus died four days ago and he remained in his grave since then. They became stunned to see with their own eyes how Lazarus walked out when Jesus called his name aloud and commanded him to come out from his grave.

By this amazing instance, God only wanted His people to reflect and realize that He is their Supreme Lord, and He has knowledge, power, and control over everything in the entire heavens and earth and therefore they should obey Jesus whom He sent to them with His commands for their guidance.

Jesus as the "Son of God" and as the "Son of Man"

It is interesting to note that the two Greek words 'pias' or 'paida' mean servant, son, or child. But while translating them into English the overly enthusiastic translators of the Bible used a capital S for "Son" when referring to Jesus, and "servant" or "son" with a lower-case s, to mean others. They did so probably without knowing what the people of Jesus' time truly meant when they called someone "Son of God," or "Son of Man."

"Son of God" refers to a righteous person

In the Jewish language, and culture a loyal, righteous, and a God-fearing person was called "Son of God". I quoted below a few verses from both parts of the Holy Bible to justify my point.

(Psalm 2:7) I [David] *will declare the decree: the LORD hath said unto me, Thou art my son; this day have I begotten thee.*

(Exodus 4:22) [To Moses] *And thou shalt say unto Pharaoh, Thus saith the LORD, Israel is my son, even my firstborn.*

(1 Chronicles 22:10) *He [Solomon] shall build a house for my name; and he shall be my son, and I will be his father.*

(Job 38:7) *When the morning stars sang together, and all the sons of God shouted for joy.*

(Matthew 3:17) *And lo a voice from heaven, saying, This is my beloved Son, in whom I am well pleased.*

(Romans 8:14) *For as many as they are led by the Spirit of God, they are the sons of God.*

The verses I quoted above do not show any difference in the status, place, or position among the sons of God. Rather, they all have been used for the most noble, righteous, obedient, and beloved servants or the messengers of God.

I also have quoted two verses from the Gospel of Mark and Luke, concerning a remark by a centurion about Jesus, after he saw him die on the cross.

(Mark 15:39) *And when the centurion, which stood over against him, saw that he [Jesus] so cried out, and gave up the ghost, he said, truly this man was the Son of God.*

(Luke 23:47) *Now when the centurion saw what was done, he glorified God, saying, certainly this was a righteous man.*

In the Gospel of Luke, the phrase "Son of God" was replaced by a "Righteous man," because, people of Jesus' time as I mentioned before, used to address a noble and righteous man as the "Son of God".

"Son of man" refers to a human being

It is interesting to note that Jesus called himself "son of man" more frequently than the "Son of God." The scholars in the Jewish language and culture tell us, people of Jesus' time used to call a human being as "son of man." According to the practice of that time, Jesus who was born and brought up in a Jewish family also called himself "son of man," though he had no human father. By "son of man" Jesus simply meant he was a human being or a man of flesh and blood. At this point, I also like to mention that Jesus referred himself as the "son of man" about eighty times whereas he mentioned himself as the "son of God" may be ten times in the Chapters 5 and 11 in the Gospel of John. In this connection, I also like to point out that as the days unfold and proceed toward more advancement, the open-minded and the truth-seeking scholars of the Holy Bible seemed to make more progress in identifying Jesus' true status, role, and mission out of those misleading names or titles. They already took care many of them either through amendments, elimination, or adding footnotes. Some amendments or elimination are also made in the most prominent and popular dogma regarding Jesus' status as the "Son of God".

"Son of God" has been eliminated from Mark 1:1 and Acts 8:37

In the narration of the New World Translation of the Holy Scriptures, the title "Son of God" has been eliminated from the Gospel of Mark 1.1.

Another important elimination regarding "Son of God" was made in Acts 8:37 in the Version of King James where Philip said to the eunuch:

"If thou believest with all thine heart, thou mayest. And he answered and said, I believe that Christ is the Son of God.

But the entire verse has now been eliminated from the New International Version of the Bible, with a footnote at the bottom of the page that tells us in brief it was found in some manuscripts. The situation got more complex, when the word "begotten" was added to the phrase "Son of God" to make Jesus' status being equal to God or as the "Savior of mankind."

"Begotten" has been removed from John 3:16

Most of my missionary friends often quoted the following verse from John 3:16 in support of their eternal life through believing in Jesus' sacrifice for the sin of man

For God so loved the world, that He gave His only Begotten Son, that whosoever believeth in him should not perish, but have everlasting life.

But the keyword "Begotten" has been removed from John 3:16, in all the modern versions of the Bible. The open-minded scholars of the Bible found the word "Begotten" came from the Greek word monogenes, which means unique or special. This describes Jesus accurately because of his miraculous birth, the miracles he performed, his crucifixion, reappearance, or his ascent to heaven alive-all these extraordinary episodes of his life, has truly made him a very unique and a special human being not only in the history of religion, but also in the history of mankind.

The Quran describes God's wrath upon them who ascribe son to Him

In fact, what the most enlightened and open-minded scholars of the Bible have now discovered on Jesus' being the 'only begotten of God' through years of their time, toil, patience, and perseverance, the Quran- the last and the final Book of God, denounced it to be a monstrous lie about fourteen hundred years ago through Jesus' testifier Muhammad. Not only that the Quran also describes God's wrath upon them who ascribe son to Him. Following verses of the Quran may be examined to verify the truth.

(17:111) [To Muhammad] *And say: Praise be to Allah Who has not taken unto Himself a son, and Who has no partner in the Sovereignty, nor He needs any protecting friend to support Him. And magnify Him with all magnificence.*

(19:88–92) *And they [the Christians] say: The Most Gracious [Allah] has begotten a son! Indeed, they have said a most monstrous lie! For which the skies are ready to burst, the earth is to split asunder and the mountains are to fall in utter ruin, that they ascribe a son to the most Gracious [Allah]. For it is not befitting to the Compassionate God that He should beget a son.*

(10:68) *They (Christians) say: 'Allah has begotten a son!' Glory be to Him! He is self-Sufficient! His is all that is in the heavens and earth! Have you any proof for what you say? Would you ascribe to Allah something about which you have no knowledge?*

The Quran has addressed Jesus as the son of Mary

Jesus' name has been used in the Quran frequently, and it has always been followed by "son of Mary." We may consider it most easy and appropriate to understand and to identify Jesus' true status by the scholars and the illiterates alike. Let us check how Jesus has been addressed in the Quran through his testifier Muhammad:

(4:171) *O people of the Book! [meaning the Christians] Do not exceed the limits in your religion, nor say of Allah anything but the truth. The Messiah Jesus, the son of Mary was no more than a Messenger of God.*

(3:45) *When the angels said, O Mary! Indeed Allah gives you the good news of a Word from Him, whose name will be the Messiah Jesus (Jesus Christ), the son of Mary, illustrious in this world and the Hereafter, and among those who are close to Allah.*

(5:75) *Christ, the son of Mary, was no more than a messenger. Many messengers had already passed away before him. His mother was a truthful woman; they both ate earthly food like other human beings. See how the revelations are made clear to them to know the reality; yet see how they ignore the truth.*

In this connection, I also like to mention that to save the people from all those fictions or fantasies about the relation of God with all His messengers, nowhere in the Quran God was addressed as the Father or His messengers as His sons. They were simply addressed as His prophets, messengers, servants, or slaves.

Finally, according to the quoted statements from both Bible and Quran, we may conclude Jesus was a unique and a special "Son of Mary" through his miraculous birth, a "Son of man," meaning a human being of flesh and blood, and above all a "Son of God" referring to a noble, chaste, and a righteous Messenger of God whom He sent last from the House of Israel for the guidance of his own people-the misguided Jews.

> *It is not befitting to the majesty of Allah that He should beget a son. Glory be to Him! When He determines a matter, He only says to it 'Be' and it is. (19:35)*

Letter 9

Trinity Was Invented After Jesus Left, He Never Taught It

For there are three that bear record in heaven, the Father, the Word and the Holy Ghost: And these three are one.

—1 John 5:7

Reverend,

As a reputed evangelist, you know very well that most of the Christians believe in the doctrine of the Trinity as an integral part of their faith related to the attainment of their salvation. But as a Muslim I already learned from the Quran that Jesus never taught it, or asked his people to worship him as God, or as one of the Gods in the Trinity. I found it true to the letter when I did not come across a single statement about it anywhere in the Gospel, not even in the entire Bible. It was then I became very much curious to know how the doctrine of the Trinity became an indispensable part of the Christian faith, if Jesus never taught it and the entire Bible had no record for it? So naturally, I saved my question for my missionary friends who used to visit me then off and on. But my question remained unanswered for a long time because most of them felt uncomfortable to talk about it, and left soon with some excuses, when I asked them how they worship three Gods as One.

For there are three that bear record in heaven (1 John 5:7)

Finally, a middle-aged white missionary lady, I would call her Mrs. Robinson, agreed to answer my question when she visited me on a Saturday morning. I asked her what the Gospel of Jesus has really said about the Trinity. In reply to my question, she opened her Bible in the King James Version, and said, "You will find it in 1 John 5:7" I also had that copy and after I opened it, she began to read.

For there are three that bear record in heaven, the Father, the Word, and the Holy Ghost: And these three are one.

After she finished reading, I said, "Please excuse me for my shortcomings,

I don't see where in this verse, you are asked to believe in the Father, the Word and the Holy Ghost as three Gods but to worship them as One?"

"It is understood."

"Will you please explain a bit?"

From her slow and laconic explanation, I came to know that Father is God as the Godhead; the Word is God as His only begotten Son Jesus; and there is also the Holy Ghost or the Holy Spirit along with them. These three are merged into one. Thus, the Christians worship one God in the union of three. But I remained in the dark as before.

So, I said to her again apologetically, "Please don't mind, it still sounds to me very confusing, because I think to be worshiped like God, Jesus and the Holy Ghost should also be like God. I mean, both Jesus and the Holy Ghost should have the same essence and attributes of God to be His equal and to deserve our worship. Right?"

Three of them are made of the same substances

"Right, and so they are. We believe the Father, the Son, and the Holy Ghost are made of the same substance, and because of that they have the same equal majesty and the glory of a fully independent God."

'But how do you know they are made of the same substance?' I was about to ask her, but I did not. I asked her instead, "But how do you worship three independent Gods as one independent God?"

"There lies the mystery. Despite of their being independent, we do not worship them separately. We worship them together as one God."

"But how is it possible? I mean, how could they maintain their independence after they become one and the same God?" I asked her again, trying to be very polite and patient.

"It is possible, because they are merged into one without losing their own independence and glory."

The way she described, it seemed to me the God of the Trinity matched more with a very mysterious, magical, or a supernatural being found in some fantasy digital movie, but it could no way match with the One Almighty God of the Judeo-Christian Faith or the God of Islam as described in both Bible and Quran.

Besides that, a series of unwanted but unavoidable questions flashed in my mind one after another. I wanted to ask her how 3 which is always 1 digit less than 4, and 1 digit more than 2, can be considered as 1?

I also wanted to know how the Father, the Son, and the Holy Ghost function as a fully independent God, while being merged into one?

Or what is the use of their being independent or having the same substance, glory, and majesty, if they cannot do anything separately? And, if they do, then what will happen to their unity?

Or how they maintained their unity, when Jesus-one of the inseparable parts of the Trinity died on the Cross and remained buried for three days? Did the Godhead and the Holy Ghost die with him, too?

Then to distract myself from the flow of those unwanted but unavoidable questions, I said to her again very politely, "Sorry, I still have no clue how these three Gods get merged into one without losing their own independence or majesty."

Trinity to be understood in three states of water

"I know it is very difficult to understand," Mrs. Robinson said, "especially for the people of other faiths. Okay, let me try to explain it with an example. Just think of water in its three different states: liquid, solid, and steam. Water is liquid, ice is solid, and air is steam. Now, what is the substance we find common in three of them?"

"Water, obviously."

"Similarly, the substance of three Gods is one and the same, just like the water is found common in its three different or independent states. I hope, now you know what it means."

"Sorry, I'm still confused, because we believe God is eternal and so is His essence and attributes. In that case, whatever His substance is, it should also remain with Him unchanged for eternity, right?"

"Sure. It is what I meant when I gave you the example of water. It also remains unchanged in its three states."

"It is true, but I don't think this example is good enough to clarify the status of Three Independent Gods being worshiped as the one or the same. Let me explain why. Ice, water, and steam can be considered separate and the same because all three are composed of the same substance. But we know very well that water does not remain the same in its three different states. For example, when water changes into ice, it loses its liquidity and when it turns into steam, it loses its liquidity and solidity both. Most important of all, water does not freeze into ice or change into steam on its own. It must go through certain states or conditions to become ice or steam, right?"

Mrs. Robinson did not answer. Looking at her serene face, I continued, "But we believe the essence, attributes or the substance of God remain unchanged under all circumstances. Nothing could affect, change, or destroy them anyway. I mean, if God adds anything new to His creation, or eliminates anything from His creation, or changes anything to something else, His substance always remains the same or intact. Don't you think so, too?"

"Sure, so what is your point?" Mrs. Robinson sounded a bit shaky.

"My point is simple. I just want to know how Jesus whom you claim to die for your sin, can be considered equal to God Who is eternal and ever-living?"

"Jesus is also eternal like his Father in heaven, because the Gospel tells us he overcame death through his resurrection. Who but God has control over life and death?"

"Sure. I have no question about that. But you also believe Jesus' resurrection took place after three days of his burial. In that case how could you claim Jesus to be eternal like God Who never dies, sleeps, or remains unconscious even for a moment?

"We believe so because after the resurrection, Jesus met with his disciples and promised to stay with them until the end of the world. Do you think, Jesus would promise so, if he were not eternal like God?"

> Teaching them to observe all things whatsoever I have commanded you. And, lo, I am with you, always, even unto the end of the world. Amen.
>
> (Matthew 28:19)

I certainly did not expect to hear it from her in support of Jesus' being eternal or equal to God. But as I needed to proceed with the topic my discussion, I said, "I know you are talking about the last verse of the last Chapter in the Gospel of Matthew, right?"

"I appreciate your memory."

"Thanks. But my memory is not that good as you think. I remember it because for the last few days, I'm trying to read the first four Gospels minutely to know how Jesus was crucified and what happened before and after that. Now, we may go back where we left."

"Sure."

"You said Jesus is eternal because he promised to stay with his disciples until the end of the world, right?"

"Yes,"

"But I think you took the apparent meaning of what Jesus said, and overlooked its inherent message. As far as I understand, Jesus did not mean to stay with them as the eternal God does. Jesus meant to stay with them to the end of the world through his spirit, morals or teaching that he left for them in the Gospel." I stopped here for a moment, and then said, "In fact, it is not only Jesus but the Prophets like Abraham, Moses, Muhammad, and other legendary figures in the history of the world, are still alive in the hearts of men through their noble acts or examples. So, what do you think of them? Are they eternal too, as God is?"

Jesus had power over entire heavens and earth

"But they are not like Jesus," Mrs. Robinson tried to oppose nicely, "None of them had power like God, but Jesus had."

"But how do you know he had power like God?"

"Jesus said it himself. He said he had power over entire heavens and earth. Okay, let me read to you. You will find it in the last chapter of Matthew, the verse is 18."

"Sure." She started reading after I opened my Bible.

And Jesus came and spoke unto them, saying, All power is given unto me in heaven and in earth.

"Do you think, Jesus could ever claim so, if he were not as powerful as God is?" Mrs. Robinson asked me straight while holding the Bible on her lap.

I read that verse before, so I said, "I think, you have overlooked one tiny but vital point that Jesus left in his claim. He told his disciples clearly that all power over the heavens and earth was given to him. It means Jesus had that power or authority only after he received it from God, not before that. In that case, how could we claim the status of the Giver and the given is one or the same?"

"Sorry. I think we are too small to understand the mystery of this relation between the Father and the Son."

'Can you please tell me where did you find the mystery when it is as clear as daylight?' I was about to ask, but I did not. From my long experience with my missionary friends, I became familiar with the pattern of their thoughts and questions. Whenever they lack reason, they try to cover it with the excuse of mystery, and when they talk about mystery, they try to avoid questions and become eager to leave. But I did not want her to leave.

So, I said to her promptly "Okay, it is for the sake of argument, I believe Jesus is eternal and as powerful as God is. But it still does not make him God, because it does not tell us whether he is as wise as God is, or he comprehends everything in his knowledge or vision as God does."

"It doesn't tell us either, he is not wise or all-knowing as God is, right?" Mrs. Miller

"Right. But Jesus made it clear through his own words and deeds that he was not All-knowing as God is. The Gospel tells us once talking to his disciples, Jesus admitted to them honestly that he was unaware of the Last Hour. He also told them no one had any knowledge of that except God. (Math 24:36) Besides that, if you read the story of the fig tree in Mark 11, you will also notice that Jesus did not know even the season of the fig. He walked to the tree to appease his hunger without knowing it had no fruit but the leaves. Don't you think, if Jesus were God or His equal, nothing could remain hidden from his knowledge or vision?"

Jesus asked his disciples to teach and baptize all nations in the name of the "Three"

"Then why Jesus commanded his disciple to baptize all nations in the name of the Father, the Son, and the Holy Ghost, if he knew he were not God or one of the Gods in the Trinity?" She asked me back instantly, but very politely.

I already read that verse several times and reflected upon it deeply to comprehend its true meaning or implication since I knew Jesus never taught the Trinity which his devoted followers now believe in his name as an indispensable part of their faith.

So, I thanked her in silence for her question and asked her casually, "Do you think, by this command, Jesus meant all nations to worship the Father, the Son, and the Holy Ghost as one God?"

"Isn't it most obvious? Otherwise, why we have been worshiping them as one God for the last two thousand years?"

"Do you think, a wrong thing turns to be right if it is believed to be right for thousands of years? No, it does not."

"May I please know what makes you so sure that it is wrong?"

From her question, I understood she was also one of them who claim the Gospel as the true account of Jesus' own words and deeds but hardly try to know what the Book has really said about him or about his teaching.

So, I told her frankly, "I'm sure for several reasons. First, Jesus cannot teach anything to his people which goes against the eternal truth of the First Commandment that he preached and practiced all through his life. Second, you will find no statement in the Gospel where Jesus was seen teaching anything about the Trinity before or after he was arrested by the Roman authority on a false charge of sedition. Third, we have no reason to doubt that Jesus taught the Trinity, but the writers of the four Gospels somehow forgot to mention it. Fourth, we also have no chance to guess that Jesus taught it to his disciples in secret or in private when no one was around them. I think so, because while talking to the High priest about certain charges against him, Jesus told him clearly that he did not teach them anything in secret. Rather, he always talked to them openly."

> *"The high priest then asked Jesus of his disciples, and of his doctrine. Jesus answered him, I spoke openly to the world; I ever taught in the synagogue, and in the temple, whither the Jews always resort; and in secret have I said nothing. Why asks thou me? Ask them which heard me, what I have said unto them: behold, they know what I said."*
> *(John 18:19–21)*

"Then why Jesus asked his disciples to baptize all nations in the name of the Father, the Son, and the Holy Ghost, if he did not mean to worship them as one God?" Mrs. Robinson repeated her question trying to hide her frustration.

"If you don't mind listening, I can try to explain it as I understood myself."

"Sure. I'll be happy to know."

"Thanks. As far as I understand, baptism is a kind of celebration that you generally observe marking your child's admission in the Church or giving him a name, right?"

"Right."

"I also have heard that the Baptist of the Churches conducts this ceremony by dipping the child in water or by sprinkling him with water."

"Yes, a child needs to go through this kind of stuff."

"I also learned that baptism is not a mere ceremony. It has some inner or deeper meaning than admitting the child in the Church or giving his name. It also means to bring some changes in the heart of the child with the light or the spirit of faith so that he could love and obey God unconditionally as did Jesus and his true followers. For this reason, it is believed that baptism works better upon the older children when they understand the true meaning of the ceremony. Right?"

"Yes." Mrs. Robinson said in brief.

"Now based on that explanation, we can rightly assume that Jesus did not want his disciples to teach and baptize all nations in the name of the Father, the Son and the Holy Ghost to worship them as One God. He asked them to teach the people of all nations about the true status of God, the Son, and the Holy Spirit so that they never worshiped them as One God, when the false prophets would come and teach them so in his name. But Jesus' ascent to heaven was imminent. He had no time to give them long advice or instruction. He chose two brief instructions to cover everything that he preached and practiced himself following the footsteps of all his predecessors."

The status of the Father, the Son and the Holy Ghost is not the same

"By the first instruction," I continued, "Jesus wanted his disciples to baptize or to enlighten the people of all nations of what they really knew about God Whom he used to call his Father in heaven and him as His son. Jesus wanted them to teach the people about his role and mission as a messenger of God. He also wanted them to teach the people who was the Holy Ghost or the Holy Spirit along with his true status in the eyes of God. Jesus assigned his disciples with this job because they learned from him very well that the status of God was the highest of all and it could never be equal to Jesus whom He made special through his miraculous birth and chose as His Messenger for the guidance of his people. Similarly, they also knew perfectly well the Holy Spirit was the Angel Gabriel and he was the Chief of all angels. They also knew he was a noble Messenger of God, and his job was to convey the words of God to His appointed messengers on earth, and to help them to carry out their prophetic mission. Jesus' disciples also heard and knew the Holy Spirit appeared to Virgin Mary by the command of God to convey to her about the birth of his son Jesus. They also knew it was the same Holy Spirit who helped Jesus to perform his stunning miracles, to rise him up from his tomb, and finally to raise him up to heaven. In other word, both Jesus and the Holy Spirit were but the appointed slaves or servants of God who tried to accomplish their assigned job by His command. Do you think Mrs. Robinson," I asked her last "With this clear knowledge and understanding about the status of the Father, the Son and the Holy Spirit, Jesus' disciples would ever think that their master asked them to baptize all nations in the name of the Three to believe and worship them as One God?"

In reply to my question, Mrs. Robinson asked me very politely, "Will you mind if I leave now. I have to take my father to his dentist."

"Sure. Family should come first."

The statement in 1John 5:7 has been discarded as unauthentic

Reverend, when Mrs. Robinson read the verse in 1John 5:7 in support of the Trinity, I did not know then that it was already discarded from the Revised Standard Version of the Bible as an unauthorized addition to the Greek text of the New Testament. When I first came to know about it, I tried to verify the truth in the Zondervan New International Version Bible, where it has mentioned in a footnote that the verses 7-8 in the chapter of 1John, was not found in any Greek manuscript before the fourteenth century. The Holman Christian Standard Bible has also found it as an unauthorized addition to the Greek text of the New Testament. In this connection, I also like to remind you that Saint Paul- the founder of the Modern Christianity and the writer of the last seventeen books of the New Testament, did not mention anything about the Trinity in any of his books. In that case, the most obvious question is how the Trinity became an integral part of the Christian faith, if it was not taught by Jesus or by any of his disciples or even by Paul who claimed to learn everything from Jesus though his vision?

The Trinity was a manmade product approved by the Council of Nicaea

While looking for the answer, I came across with some authentic and well-researched books where I found the doctrine of the Trinity was a manmade product and it was approved by the council of Nicaea and it became an indispensable part of Christian faith about 325 years after Jesus' ascent to heaven. The doctrine of Trinity was first presented by Athanasius- an Egyptian deacon from Alexandria and was accepted by the Council of Nicaea in 325 CE. It is called the Creed of Nicaea. I have quoted below some of it from the report accepted or approved by the Council.

Whoever wishes to be saved must, above all, keep the Catholic faith.

"This is what the Catholic faith teaches: We worship one God in the Trinity and the Trinity in unity. We distinguish among the persons, but we do not divide the substance. For the Father is a distinct person; the Son is a distinct person; and the Holy Spirit is a distinct person. Still the Father and the Son and the Holy Spirit have One divinity, equal glory, and coeternal majesty. What the Father is, the Son is, and the Holy Spirit is. … The Father is eternal, the Son is eternal, and the Holy Spirit is eternal. Nevertheless, there are not three eternal beings, but one eternal being. … Likewise, the Father is omnipotent, the Son is omnipotent, and the Holy Spirit is omnipotent. Yet there are not three omnipotent beings, but one omnipotent being. Thus, the Father is God, the Son is God, and the Holy Spirit is God. But they are not three gods but one God. … For according to the Christian truth, we must profess that each of the persons individually is

God; and according to Christian religion we are forbidden to say that there are three gods or lords. But the entire three persons are co-eternal and co-equal with one another."

Christian Truth is different from Christian Religion

Reverend, it is interesting to note that according to the manifesto of the Council of Nicaea, the Christian truth is different from the Christian religion. The Christian truth wants its adherents to profess each of the three persons—the Father, the Son, and the Holy Spirit as being a separate and independent God. But the Christian religion forbids its adherents to call them three Gods and to regard the 'three' being one, co-eternal and coequal to one another.

This is how the eternal truth in the Everlasting or the First Commandment of God (Gen. 17:7, Duet. 6:4-5, Mark. 12:29-30), which was pure and pristine monotheism, got contaminated with the pagan practice of polytheism and became assimilated with the Christian faith in the name of Jesus.

The Trinity was rejected by the Unitarian Christians

But we have no reason to believe that Jesus' true followers, the Unitarian Christians, or the worshipers of One True God, accepted the doctrine of the Trinity as they were commanded to do by the polytheist Roman Authority at that time. According to the authentic report of the historians and open-minded religious scholars, we came to know they rejected it at once to be wrong, inappropriate, and above all, as a grave sin of blasphemy. When the Authority or the Council failed to justify their doctrine through logic, evidence, or acceptable explanation, they tried to force them to accept it blindly. Not only that they also began to arrest, torture, burn, and to crucify them inhumanly who dared to oppose the council or to criticize their doctrine in public. Many of them were also reported to leave their home and hearth and began to live in the desolate forest or in the caves of mountains only to save their faith from the tyranny of their oppressors. But, it is also a fact that by the end of the fourth century, the doctrine of the Trinity became assimilated as an indispensable part of the Christian faith, and since then, the devoted followers of Jesus Christ have been worshiping God in the union of three by ignoring the crystal-clear message of the First Commandment that Jesus taught them himself and which they still find in the Gospel-the Book they love to claim as a true account of Jesus' own words and deeds.

Interestingly, the Christians of the Modern world-both educated and illiterate also accepted the Trinity as their key to salvation without ever trying to know how Jesus and the Holy Spirit could be equal to the Eternal and the Almighty God Who was their Creator-Lord and the Disposer of all affairs in the entire heavens and earth? Or, why they should accept this kind of ambiguous, unjust and unacceptable doctrine made by men against the clear, consistent and the everlasting command of God preached and practiced by all His messengers who were sent before Jesus? Now, there is no oppression from any quarter at least in the matter of religion, but Jesus' devoted followers chose to remain oblivious to what Jesus said to them warning about the arrival of the false prophets along with their false doctrines and what might happen to them, if they believe and follow them blindly. (Matthew 7:15,21; 24:4-5; 15:9,13-14; 5:9)

The Quran has denounced the Trinity as a clear blaspheme against the oneness of God

The Quran, which God revealed to Jesus' Testifier Muhammad about six hundred years after his ascent to heaven, has denounced the doctrine of the Trinity as a clear blaspheme against the oneness of God. There are many oft-repeated verses in the Quran that tell us clearly Jesus never asked his people to worship him as God or as one of the Gods in the Trinity. Rather, he always asked his people to worship none but One God as he did himself following the faith and practices of all his predecessors. I have quoted below a few of them from different parts of the Holy Quran to justify my claim.

(4:171) O people of the Book! [Meaning the Christians] Do not transgress on the limits of your religion. Speak nothing but the truth about Allah. The Messiah Jesus, the son of Mary was no more than a Messenger of Allah and His word 'Be' which He bestowed upon Mary and a Spirit from Him. So, believe in Allah and His Messenger and do not say Trinity. Stop saying that. Allah is only One Deity.

(5:72) Certainly, they have disbelieved who say: "Allah is Christ-the son of Mary while Christ himself said, "O children of Israel! Worship Allah; my Lord and your Lord.' whoever commits shirk [to worship God in association with others], Allah will deny him the paradise, and the hellfire will be his home"

(5:73) They disbelieve who say: "God is one of the 'three' in a Trinity." For,

there is no god except One God. If they desist not from what they say, verily a grievous chastisement will befall the disbelievers among them.

(9:31) *They [Jews and Christians] have taken their rabbis and their priests to be their lords beside Allah and so they did with Messiah, the son of Mary, though they were commanded [in the Torah and the Gospel] to worship none but One God, besides Whom there is none worthy of worship. Exalted is He from having partners they associate with Him.*

Sometimes I think, if the members of the Council of Nicaea had any idea that God would send His last prophet Muhammad about two hundred fifty years after testifying of Jesus's true status, clearing his name from all the lies and falsehood that they imposed upon him, and protecting his honor along with his virgin mother Mary in His everlasting Guidebook-the Quran, they would have thought twice before they dared venturing into the words of God or demeaning the sanctity of any of His appointed messengers.

> (3:79–80) *It is not possible for a man whom Allah has given the Book, the Wisdom and the Prophethood that he would say to the people: Worship me instead of Allah. On the contrary he would say: Be worshipers of your Lord in accordance with the Holy Book that you have been teaching and reading. Nor would he command you to take the angels and the prophets as your Lords. Would he order you to disbelieve after you have surrendered to God?*

Letter 10

Some Misunderstood or Misinterpreted Statements of Jesus

That is why, I speak to them in parables: Though seeing, they do not see; though hearing, they do not hear or understand. And in them is fulfilled the prophecy of Isaiah;" You will be ever hearing but never understanding; you will be ever seeing but never perceiving.

—Matthew 13:13–14

Reverend,

In this letter, I intend to describe some of the statements from the Gospel where most of the devoted Christians find clear indication to believe and worship Jesus as God or along with God. But I think if they study them with an open mind and ponder over them deeply, they will find the true meaning of those statements of Jesus got somehow distorted, after he left. I have of course tried to justify my point with proper evidence from the Gospel-the Book they believe themselves as the true account of Jesus' own words and deeds.

Before I begin, I should mention first about two important criteria of Jesus' way or style of teaching. An attentive reader of the Gospel will find his teaching both transparent and metaphoric in nature. The message of some of his statements is plain, simple, and easily understood by the illiterates and the scholars alike. But the message of some of his statements is too complicated for the common and ordinary people to grasp their inherent meaning or implication because Jesus expressed them in metaphor. Let me clarify this difference with Jesus' own statements in the Gospel.

Clear and Conclusive Statements made by Jesus

(Mark 12:29–30) *And Jesus answered him [a Jewish scribe], The first of all the commandments is, Hear, O Israel, the LORD our GOD is ONE LORD: And thou shalt love the LORD thy GOD with all thy heart, and with all thy soul, and with all thy mind and with all thy strength: this is the first commandment.*

(Matthew 19:26) *Jesus looked at them and said, with man this is impossible, but with God all things are possible.*

(Mark11:22) *Have faith in God, Jesus answered.*

Metaphoric and misunderstood statements of Jesus

(John 10:30) *I and my Father are one.*

(John 14:6) *I am the way, the truth, and the life: no man cometh unto the Father, but by me.*

(John 14:9) *Whoever has seen me has seen the Father.*

I may now try to explain those complicated or misinterpreted statements of Jesus as I understood myself from the study of the Gospel as well as other authentic books written by the eminent Muslim and non-Muslim scholars- both old and modern.

Let me begin first with the verse 30 in John 10, which my missionary friends loved to quote to prove Jesus and God are one and the same.

I and my Father are one (John 10:30).

Jesus said it when he faced an unpleasant encounter with the Jews on Solomon's porch in the temple of Jerusalem. They gathered around him and began to ask him persistently to tell them whether he was the Christ or not. (John 10:22–38) But Jesus, being an inspired messenger of God, knew very well why they were insisting him on telling something which they already knew to be true. He knew that the Jews did not want to accept him as the promised Messiah of God because of their drifting away from the Laws of the Torah that Moses received from God. He also knew the High priest who was then working for the Roman Authority behind the door, was motivating them to reject him and his teaching to be false and blasphemous. So, to expose their dubious role Jesus said to them certain things that made the intention of their hearts quite clear.

In reply to their enquiry about him or his mission, Jesus said to them a little sarcastically, that they would surely have known him by this time, if they were his sheep, meaning his true followers. By this statement, he told them indirectly but undoubtedly who he really was and why he was sent for.

> *I am not sent but unto the lost sheep*
> *of the house of Israel.*
> *(Matthew 15:24).*

Then, he volunteered some information to them about his disciples' unconditional faith and submission to God and to His commands that He sent through him for their guidance. In addition to that, Jesus also mentioned to them that in return to his disciples' absolute faith and submission to God, he had ensured eternal life for them. At this point, some of my young missionary friends, a college girl who knew I do not believe in Jesus' deity, asked me once how could he ensure eternal life for his disciples if he were not God?

I told her Jesus was a true messenger of God and because of that, he knew perfectly well what the people are required to do to have an eternal life in heaven. So he had no doubt in his mind that God would bless all his disciples with eternal life because they had unconditional faith in Him, and they also tried to live their life by His commands which he taught them. As Jesus helped them to have eternal life through his teaching, advice, and guidance, he claimed that it was him (as if), who gave them eternal life. As far as I remember, my young missionary friend-a college girl, did not oppose me when I explained my point to her.

But the Jews who were listening to Jesus, however felt no interest about his disciples or his giving eternal life to them. They became vigilant instantly and began to throw stones at him the moment they heard him say: I and my Father are one.

My Father, which gave them me was greater than all (John 10:29)

They took his statement as a grave sin of blaspheme against One True God and it made them so angry and upset that they totally forgot what Jesus said to them only a moment before he made that comment. While admiring his most obedient, humble and God-fearing disciples, Jesus said to the Jews: *My Father, which gave them me, is greater than all; and no man is able to pluck them out of my Father's hand.* (John 10:29).

After this clear and open confession of Jesus about God's being greater than all, he certainly did not mean he and his Father in the Heaven had the same level or status when he told the Jews I and my Father are one. They might have pondered over it and look for its inherent meaning if their mind was not set already to oppose him with the charge of blaspheme.

At this point, I can't help myself thinking that the same statement in John 10:30 which made the suspicious Jews to throw stones at Jesus with the charge of blasphemy, made his own devoted followers to believe and worship him as God or along with God by forsaking the eternal truth of the First Commandment that Jesus preached and practiced himself all through his life.

We may now go back to see how Jesus handled the Jews who began to throw stone at him for his comment in John 10:30. He tried to bring the hostile Jews back to their senses by reminding them of a verse in the Old Testament, where God addressed His messengers as gods.

> *I have said, Ye are gods; and all of you are children of the Most High. (Psalm 82:6)*

Jesus mentioned this verse to remind the Jews about the status of his predecessors in the eyes of God. They were addressed by God as "gods" and His "children" so that people believe and obey them as His chosen or favorite persons whom He sent to them for their guidance. With this reminder, Jesus wanted the Jews to believe and accept him as one of them who were sent before him with the words of God. If Jesus truly meant he was the "Son of God" or he and God were one and the same, then why would he compare his status with his predecessors? At this point, it is also interesting to note that in Psalm 82:6, "gods" is written with a lowercase 'g,' but for whatever reason, it began with an uppercase when it was put in Jesus' mouth in John 10:34.

The Father is in me, and I in him (John 10:38).

The Jews despite of their suspicion against Jesus' role and mission, might have accepted his explanation but could not, because while talking to them about his works which he always tried to do by the command of God, Jesus said to them again: *that ye may know, and believe, that the Father is in me, and I in him.*

The Jews, who were too impatient or too shallow because of their low faith, or personal gain, failed to understand the inherent meaning in Jesus' words, and misunderstood him again completely. They became more aggressive and tried to get hold of him, but Jesus managed to escape to a safer place, as a sensible human being would have done against the assault of a hostile mob.

True meaning or significance of Jesus' statement in John 10:30 and 38

We may now check the True meaning or significance of Jesus' statement in John 10:30 and 38, where he said to the Jews *I and my Father are one, or the Father is in me and I in him?*

In fact, verses 30 and 38 are metaphorical in nature. Jesus tried to convey to his people something different or deeper than its apparent meaning. To understand the inherent message of his metaphorical speech, we need to know first some key points of his teaching.

First, Jesus wanted his people to understand his intimate and unique relation with God Whom he often called his Father in Heaven and him as His Son.

Second, in many places of the Gospel, Jesus said to his people repeatedly that he was a Prophet of God and he was sent to them for their guidance.

Third, many a time, he was seen to remind his people that he never said or did anything but by the command of God.

Fourth, sometimes Jesus was found to express his frustration about the low faith and lack of understanding of his disciples.

Fifth, Jesus made several prophecies about the false prophets who would come after him with their false doctrines to misguide his people from his teaching. He also made it clear what might happen to them, if they reject his teaching and follow the invented doctrines of men.

Sixth, Jesus also made a series of clear prophecies about the arrival of his Advocate or Comforter who would testify of his true status, glorify him and also guide his misled people to the eternal truth of the First Commandment of God that he taught them himself.

Keeping all those points in view, no sensible person would ever believe Jesus meant himself God or His equal when he said to the Jews, *I and my Father are one, or My Father is in me and I in him*. Jesus told them so to mean he was one or same with God in fulfilling His mission that He entrusted upon him. The mission was to proclaim the worship of none but One God among his people as did all his predecessors before him. In many places of the Gospel, Jesus also admitted himself openly that he did everything by the command of God and for the sake of His pleasure. (John 8:28-29; 12:49) In other word, he felt himself one or same with God in fulfilling His mission or purpose on earth. Following points may also be taken into consideration in support of that.

To convince the Jews about his role and mission on earth, Jesus said to them: *For the works that the Father has given me to finish-the very works that I am doing-testify that the Father has sent me (John 5:36)*

And this is eternal life: that they know you, the only true God, and Jesus Christ, whom you have sent (John 17:3).

Despite of that clear admission from Jesus himself, if his devoted followers like to believe he was God or His equal for his saying I and my Father are one, or My Father is in me and I in him, I would request them to read the supplication of Jesus that he made to God fervently for his disciples and other believers in John 17:20-21.

In a heart rendering supplication to God, Jesus is seen to beg Him most humbly: *Neither pray I for these (his disciples) alone, but for them also which shall believe on me through their word; That they all may be one; as thou, Father, art in me, and I in thee, that they also may be one in us: that the world may believe that thou hast sent me (John17:21).*

Exact number of God: One, Two, Three, or unlimited

Reverend, while reading the contents of Jesus' prayer to God, any sensible and open-minded reader might ask in wonder if Jesus meant himself God for his saying, *I and my Father are one, or the Father is in me, and I in him*, then his devoted followers should also worship his twelve disciples and other believers in him as God after their being united with Jesus and his Father as one. There is also the Holy Ghost or the Holy Spirit to add with them, too. At this point, I think you or other devoted followers of Jesus should not feel offended, if we ask them about the exact numbers of Gods that they worship as One God. Is it One and Only God as Jesus taught them in the First Commandment? Or is it 'Two' that they discovered from Jesus' saying to the Jews, I and my Father are one, or the Father is in me, *and I in him?* Or is it 'Three' that they were forced to believe by the Council of Nicaea in 325 CE after Jesus left? Or the number of their Gods are 'Unlimited' after Jesus' prayer in John 17:20-21 was fulfilled by God? This type of undesirable but unavoidable questions are bound to occur, when people worship God according to the invented doctrines of men by ignoring the eternal truth of His guidance which they still find recorded in their own Holy Book. (Duet 6:4-5); (2 Samuel 7:22); (Isaiah 45:21); (Matthew 4:10); and (Mark 12:29-30)

We shall now try to examine other statements of Jesus in the Gospel where his followers find clear proofs to worship him as God or along with God.

I am the way, the truth, and the life (John 14:6)

In the statement of John 14:6, Jesus has claimed: *I am the way, the truth, and the life: no man cometh unto the Father but by me.*

My missionary friends used to quote this verse in support of Jesus' being equal to God, while I used to oppose them saying that it were not Jesus alone, all the chosen messengers of God were in fact the way, the truth, and the life to their people. They were called so because God made Himself and His Path known to their people through His appointed messengers. It is through the teaching and guidance of their respective messengers, people came to know about the existence of One True Eternal God as their Creator, Protector, Guide, and the Disposer of all their affairs. It is through them their people learned about their eternal life after death, the existence of heaven and hell, and the Day of Judgment. They also learned from them what they needed to do to meet God in heaven or to have their eternal life. Similarly, they also learned from their respective messengers what they needed to forsake to save them from the fire of hell. In brief, people can expect to meet with God in heaven only through keeping His commands that He sent to them through their respective messengers. In that sense, Jesus was right, if he claimed, *I am the way, the truth, and the life: no man cometh unto the Father but by me.*

I think, it is like meeting with the US President in the White House through his personal attaché who may claim no one could meet the President without him. Does it mean he claims so to mean he and the President of America are one and the same?

He that hath seen me, hath seen the Father (John 14:9)

It is another metaphorical statement of Jesus which my missionary friends used to quote in support of Jesus' being equal to God. Some of them told me Jesus meant himself God when Philip-one of his disciples said to him, *Lord, show us the Father and that will be enough for us,* and in reply to that, Jesus answered: *Don't you know me, Philip, even after I have been among you such a long time? Anyone who has seen me has seen the Father. How can you say, show us the Father?* (John 14:9)

But after I read Jesus' answer to Philip minutely, I felt there is a subtle reproach in what he said. Jesus did not expect this question from one of his close companions who knew him so well and what he preached and practiced himself in the name of God, how he prayed to God, and how he taught them to pray, or guided them to His Path.

Not only that Jesus also made it clear to them that they could never hear the voice of God nor see His shape (John 5:37). In that case, it is very much expected Jesus could not appreciate Philip's question when he asked him straight to show his Father to them. We may now check what Jesus really meant when he said *anyone who has seen me has seen the Father.*

By this claim, Jesus actually meant that his disciples who truly followed the Path of God through keeping His commands that he taught them, would surely go to heaven where they would see God with their own eyes. As Jesus believed they would see God in heaven because of their complete obedience to him and to his guidance, he told Philip, *He that hath seen me, hath seen the Father.* In other word, if they did not know him, obey him, or follow his guidance, they had no chance to see God in heaven.

If Jesus really meant himself God by this claim, then why did he teach his disciples *no one could ever hear His voice or see His shape?* (John 5:37). I mean if Jesus were God, this description does not match with him at all, because he was heard and seen by multitudes when he lived among them. At this point, a sensible person might like to know about their consequence who saw Jesus with their own eyes, but declined to obey him or follow his path? Or what about them who believe and obey his path, but never saw him?

Take heart, son; your sins are forgiven (Matthew 9:2)

My Christian friends believe no one could forgive our sin except God. Since Jesus forgave the sin of the man sick with paralysis, they took him for God without considering his other drawbacks.

The man in question was paralyzed with an incurable disease, and he was a sinner, too. After he suffered for a long time, God out of His own mercy wished to make him free from both his sin and sickness. But He wanted to do it through Jesus to glorify him before the eyes of the Jews who were suspicious of his role and mission as His promised Messiah. So, Jesus was empowered by God to cure the man from his sickness as well as to forgive his sin.

If Jesus really knew he was God, and he could cure the man and forgive his sin like God, he would cure and forgive him like God and did not need any announcement or publicity to do it. Jesus' true followers knew very well that he used to do those stunning miracles being inspired by God. (Matthew 9:8; John 3:2; 5:19- 20; 11:4). If he were God, he could perform those miracles on his own anytime or anywhere he pleased. But the Gospel tells us that except for healing a few sick people by the touch of his hand, Jesus was unable to perform any powerful work in his hometown (Mark 6:5). Not only that he also failed to restore eyesight to a blind man at the first attempt and needed a second try to cure him. (Mark 8:23-25) If Jesus were God, as his devoted followers claim about him, his power would never fail, and he would not need a second try to cure the blind.

Before Abraham was, I am (John 8:58)

It is another misunderstood or misinterpreted statement of Jesus where he said, *Verily, verily, I say unto you, before Abraham was, I am.*

Jesus said it to the Jews who were still suspicious of his true status or mission and were not yet ready to accept him as the promised Messiah of God.

One of my missionary friends explained that Jesus said "I am" to mean he was God, because in Exodus 3:14, God has declared His name as "I AM." So, she expected me to believe it was a clear indication in support of Jesus' being equal or co-eternal with God.

> *And God said unto Moses, I AM that I AM: and he said, thus shalt thou say unto the children of Israel, I AM hath sent me unto you. (Exodus 3:14).*

But I took it as another metaphorical statement of Jesus which had nothing to do with the "I AM" in Exodus. If Jesus really used it to mean himself God, the translators of the Bible would gladly copy each letter of it in the upper case, as we find it written in the book of Exodus. I thought it might be a slip of tongue. Jesus said, "I am" but he meant to say, "I was." But when I told it to my missionary friend, she asked me back very politely how could I explain that when we know Jesus was sent long after Abraham?

"I wish I knew how the chronology of the chosen messengers of God was maintained in the celestial world where the question of time or date does not exist. Though it is not authentic, but the Muslims in general believe," I began to explain, "God has created first the light or the spirit of Prophet Muhammad long before He created Adam, though he was sent last of all His messengers. May be, the light or the spirit of Jesus and of all his predecessors were made right after Muhammad in the similar pattern meaning from back to top which finally ended with Adam who was sent first as the father of the mankind. In that case, it would make sense if Jesus said, he was before Abraham was. So, what do you think of that?"

"I appreciate your imagination. But as a true Christian, I take my faith seriously. We only believe what Jesus has said in the Gospel."

'Do you really? Then, how could you believe that by saying "I am" Jesus claimed himself God by denouncing the eternal truth of the first commandment that he preached and practiced himself all through his life?' But keeping my question to myself, I said to her, "You are right. We should take the words of our Holy Books seriously."

Reverend, Now, a long time after that incomplete conversation with my missionary friend, I feel myself quite happy to share with you and with my other devoted Christian friends an important piece of discovery related to the claim of Jesus in John 8:58. From further study, I luckily came to know that in the Syriac Peshitta Version of the Bible, which is considered as one of the oldest known versions, John 8:58 reads, *Before Abraham was, I was.*

I wish I could also tell you how or since when this "I was" got replaced by "I AM,"-the name of the God in Exodus and then it got tagged with the name of Jesus to make him co-eternal with God!

Test of Faith: Points to ponder

While reading those small but significant narrations in the Gospel, I often felt that the Jews who misunderstood Jesus and also accused him falsely with the charge of blaspheme, can be excused for their ignorance, arrogance or for their deviation from the Laws of God. But what about Jesus' devoted followers-the Christians who have been worshiping him along with God for the last two thousand years based on those obscure statements in the Gospel while ignoring his most clear and conclusive instructions in the First Commandment?

Sometimes I have also asked myself wondering why Jesus made those metaphoric statements to mislead the people from the path of God? Didn't he tell his people repeatedly that he never said or did anything but by the command of God? If so, why God made Jesus speak like that to confuse his people which finally deviated them from His plain and simple commands preached and practiced by Jesus himself and all his predecessors before him?

I had no clear answer at that time, but now I have. Since the verses of the revealed scriptures of God are consistent and complementary to one another, I can explain it now with a statement of the Quran-the last and the final guidebook of God that He revealed upon His last Prophet Muhammad about fourteen hundred years ago.

In verse 3:7, God has said through Muhammad:

He is the One Who has revealed to you the Book. Some of its verses are decisive-they are the foundation of the Book while others are allegorical. Those whose hearts are infected with disbelief, follow the allegorical part to mislead others and give their own interpretation, seeking for its hidden meanings, but no one knows its hidden meanings except Allah. Those who are well-grounded in knowledge say: We believe in it; it is all from our Lord. But none will take heed except the people of understanding.

Reverend, if we try to reflect on the contents of the above passage of the Quran, we shall see that God wants to test the people's faith in Him or about their commitment to His Will and Command that He conveyed to them through their respective messengers. Sometimes God wants to test them through the combination of clear and confusing statements. But He also made it clear to them that people whose faith in Him is low, shallow or shaky, usually prefer to go by the self-made interpretation of those allegorical, metaphorical or unspecific verses, which eventually deviates them from His plain, simple and straight Path. But it does not deviate them who are intelligent, understanding, and true believers in God. They believe everything in the revealed scriptures comes from God, but they follow those commands which are plain, simple, and free from all confusion.

> *For I did not speak on my own, but the Father who sent me commanded me to say all that I have spoken. I know that his command leads to eternal life. So, whatever I say is just what the Father has told me to say.* (John 12:49-50)

Letter 11

Jesus Never Said or Did Anything but by the Command of God

Touch me not; for I am not yet ascended to my father: but go to my brethren and say unto them, I ascend unto my father, and your father, and to my God, and to your God.

—John 20:17

Reverend,

In my last letter, I have tried to explain those statements of Jesus that were metaphoric in nature. But they were misunderstood or misinterpreted to such an extent that his followers began to worship him as God or along with God by ignoring the crystal clear instruction of His First Commandment that Jesus preached and practiced himself all through his life. In fact, there is no statement in the entire Gospel where Jesus said he was God, or God Incarnate, or one of the Gods in the Trinity and he should be worshiped as God or along with God. Rather, he left for us countless statements in the Gospel where he made his own status distinctly clear from the unparalleled and unattainable status of God. I have narrated some of them in support of my claim.

God is greater than all and I (10:29; 14:28)

In the following verses of the Gospel, Jesus tells his people that God or his Father in heaven, is greater than all and him, too.

(John 10:29) *My Father, which gave them me, is greater than all.*

(John 14:28) *....If ye loved me, ye would rejoice, because I said, I go unto the Father: For my Father is greater than I.*

(John 13:16) *Very truly I tell you, no servant is greater than his master, nor is a messenger greater than the one who sent him.*

God sent Jesus for the guidance of his own people

From many of the verses in the Gospel, I have quoted below only a few of them where Jesus is seen pleading his people to believe him being sent by God for their guidance and to fulfill His purpose on earth through keeping

His commands.

(Matthew 15:24) *But he [Jesus] answered and said, I am not sent but unto the lost sheep of the house of Israel.*

(Luke 4:43) *And he [Jesus] said unto them, I must preach the kingdom of God to other cities also: for therefore am I sent.*

(John 5: 36) *For the works that the Father has given me to finish-the very works that I am doing-testify that the Father has sent me.*

(John 9:4) *I must work the works of him [God] that sent me.*

(John 12:44) *Jesus cried and said, he that believeth in me, believeth not on me, but on him that sent me.*

(Mark 9:37) *Whoever welcomes one of these little children in my name welcomes me; and whoever welcomes me does not welcome me but the one who sent me.*

(John 17:3) *Now this is eternal life: that they know you; the only true God, and Jesus Christ, whom you have sent.*

(John 17:25) *Righteous Father, though the world does not know you, I know you, and they know that you have sent me.*

Now the question is, if Jesus and God were one and the same, why would he insist his people to believe he was sent by God for their guidance and to strive for His cause.

Jesus never said or did anything but by the command of God.

In the following verses of the Gospel, Jesus made it clear to all that he submitted himself completely to the will and the command of God, and he never said or did anything but by His command.

(John 8:28–29) *Then Jesus said unto them, when ye have lifted up the son of man, then shall ye know that I am he, and that I do nothing of myself; but as my father hath taught me, I speak of these things. And he that sent me is with me: the Father hath not left me alone; for I do always those things that please him.*

(John 12:49–50) *For, I did not speak on my own, but the Father who sent me commanded me to say all that I have spoken. I know that his command leads to eternal life. So, whatever I say is just what the Father has told me to say.*

Jesus not only followed the commands of God himself he also called his people to obey him and follow his commands that he received from

God for their guidance. He also made it clear to them about the reward in obeying the commands of God, and the punishment for their being disobedient to Him. (Mt. 5:19; John 8:32, 14:15)

Jesus in appreciation of God's overall power, judgment, and forgiveness

The Gospel also tells us about Jesus' utmost appreciation for God's overall power, judgment, and forgiveness. It confirms indirectly but undoubtedly that Jesus was not an inseparable part of God or His equal as his devoted followers still claim about him. Rather, he was a man of flesh and blood along with some human weakness, ignorance, and shortcoming despite of his being righteous and a noble Prophet of God. Jesus knew that, too and because of that he made several statements in the Gospel where he tried to make his people understand that it is only God Who deserves their unquestioning faith, obedience, appreciation, and worship. I have described some of them in the following sub-titles to highlight the points of my argument.

Jesus does not forgive; his Father in heaven does.

(Luke 23:34) *Then said Jesus, Father, Father, forgive them; for they know not what they do.*

Jesus had no place to lay his head.

(Luke 9:58) *Jesus replied, Foxes have dens, and birds have nests, but the Son of man has no place to lay his head.*

There are plenty of verses in both Bible and Quran, where we have been told repeatedly that God is the Creator and the Controller of the entire heavens and earth and everything that exists in them, belong to Him. But here we see Jesus whom his people worship as God, admits himself openly that he had no place to lay his head, when foxes and birds have.

Jesus needed strength from heaven

(Luke 22:43) *And there appeared an angel unto him (Jesus) from heaven, strengthening him.*

At this point, I also like to mention that there is a similar verse in the

Quran in 5:110, where God says to Jesus, *O Jesus, son of Mary! Recall my favor upon you and to your mother, how I strengthened you with the Holy Spirit.*

Reverend, could you please give us an acceptable explanation why Jesus needed strength from an angel, if he were God or His equal as you claim? You do not have any, but we have many to prove Jesus needed that strength to accomplish his assignment that God entrusted upon him for the guidance of his people.

Jesus was ignorant of the last hour

(Mark 13:32) *But about that day or hour no one knows, not even the angels in heaven, nor the Son, but only the Father.*

In the above quoted statement, Jesus is seen to include himself with the angels and the rest of mankind who are ignorant of the Last Hour. Jesus would never admit of his ignorance about such an important or major event like the end of this existing world, if he were God Who is known to encompass everything in His knowledge or vision. But he did not mind to admit his ignorance because he was a true messenger of God, and like all the messengers before him and Muhammad who arrived after him, he also knew no one was aware of the Last Hour except God.

Jesus prayed to God more when he was in anguish

(Mark 14:32) *They went to a place … and Jesus said to his disciples, Sit here, while I pray.*

(Luke 6:12) *And it came to pass in those days, that he went out into a mountain to pray, and continued all night in prayer to God.*

(Luke 22:44) *And being in anguish, he prayed more earnestly, and his sweat was like drops of blood falling to the ground.*

In the quoted verses above, it is clear to all that Jesus often prayed to God, and he prayed to Him more when he was in distress. At this point, a sensible reader might ask in wonder, does the God of mankind ever go through any kind of distress or agony as a man does? Or does God ever pray to Himself to remove His distress or to fulfill any of His desires? Or, if Jesus and God were one and the same and in distress, who prayed to whom to get rid of that?

Jesus taught his disciples how to pray to God

According to the description in Luke 11:1–4, Jesus was praying in a certain place. When he finished, one of his disciples said to him, Lord, teach us to pray, just as John (referring to John-the Baptist) taught his disciples. And he (Jesus) said unto them, When ye pray, say:

Our Father which art in heaven, hallowed be thy name. Thy kingdom come. Thy will be done, as in heaven, so in earth. Give us day by day our daily bread. And forgive us our sins; for we also forgive everyone that is indebted to us. And lead us not into temptation; but deliver us from evil.

From Jesus' teaching to his disciples how to pray to God, it goes without saying that he believed himself God was their only Lord, their Creator, Provider, Protector, the Redeemer of their sin, as well as their True Guide, Savior and the Disposer of all affairs in the entire heavens and earth, and it is what his disciples learned from him. In that case, the question of claiming Jesus as God or worshiping him along with God does not arise at all.

Jesus became vulnerable as he came closer to death

(Matthew 26:39, 42) *Going a little farther, he (Jesus) fell with his face to the ground and prayed, "My father, if it is possible, may this cup be taken from me. Yet not as I will, but as you will."*

He went away a second time and prayed, "My father, if it is not possible for this cup to be taken away unless I drink it, may your will be done."

In both the verses I quoted above, Jesus' state of mind has been expressed clearly. First, as a common and an ordinary human being and then as a true messenger of God. As a man of flesh and blood, Jesus expressed his anguish and vulnerability in a crucial moment like facing death on the Cross. Then as a dedicated servant of God, he submitted himself completely to His will and command and became ready to accept gracefully what his Lord has desired or destined for him.

Jesus felt himself deserted of God's mercy at his last moment

(Matthew 27:46) *About three in the afternoon Jesus cried out in a loud voice, "Eli, Eli, lama sabachthani?"(which means "My God, my God, why have you forsaken me"?)*

Reverend, you may agree or not, but this one statement of Jesus is enough to prove he was not God or his equal, but a mortal human being. Though, we find him to submit to God's will and command completely, he could not help himself feeling deserted of His mercy, and expressing his grievances to Him openly, when he found his death on the Cross was imminent.

Jesus' own statements tell us clearly he could no way be equal to God

There are many statements in the Gospel where Jesus made it clear to all that he could no way be equal to God or his Father in heaven. I have quoted below a few of them with a question who is that God Jesus often mentioned to his people or invoked himself?

(Mark 12:29–30) *Hear, O' Israel; the Lord our God is one Lord: And thou shalt love the Lord thy God with all thy heart, and with all thy soul, and with all thy mind, and with all thy strength:*

(Luke 4:8) *And Jesus answered and said unto him, Get thee behind me, Satan: for it is written, thou shalt worship the Lord thy God, and Him only shalt thou serve.*

(John 20:17) *Touch me not; for I am not yet ascended to my Father: but go to my brethren and say unto them, I ascend unto my Father, and your Father, and to my God, and to your God.*

(Matthew 5:48) *Be ye therefore perfect, even as your Father which is in heaven is perfect.*

(Matthew 11:25) *At that time, Jesus said, "I praise you, Father, Lord of heaven and earth, because you have hidden these things from the wise and the learned, and revealed them to little children."*

(Matthew 19:17) *….. There is none good but one, that is, God.*

(Mark 10:27) *And Jesus looking upon them said, With men it is impossible, but not with God: for with God all things are possible.*

(Mark 13:32) *But about that day or hour no one knows, not even the angels in heaven, nor the Son, but only the Father.*

(Mark 11:22) *"Have faith in God." Jesus answered.*

(John 8:40) *As it is, you are looking for a way to kill me, a man who has told you the truth that I heard from God.*

(Matthew 27:46) *About three in the afternoon Jesus cried out in a loud voice, "Eli, Eli, lama sabachthani?"(which means "My God, my God, why have you forsaken me"?)*

Jesus' miraculous birth in Support of his being equal to God

One of my young missionary friends, a very smart and intelligent college student tried to convince me once about Jesus' deity because of his miraculous birth. In reply to that I wanted to tell her the question of birth whether it is normal or miraculous does not apply to God Who is Omnipotent, Omniscient, and Self-sufficient. But I did not. I simply told her Adam's birth was more miraculous than Jesus' birth without a father, because Adam had neither father nor mother, and he did not have to go through the normal procedure of childbirth like the rest of us. I also read to her what God has said in the Quran about Jesus' birth. .

> *In fact, the example of the birth of Jesus in the sight of God is like the example of Adam who had no father and no mother. He created him out of dust and then said to him: 'Be' and he was.*
> *(Quran 3:59)*

Looking at her impassive face, I told her again, "Okay, if the instance from the Quran does not impress you that much, let me give you an example from your own Holy Bible. You will find it in the book of Hebrew- first three verses in chapter 7. I'm sure," I said to her while turning the pages of my Bible, "You will find it more miraculous than Jesus' birth without a father."

I began to read to her after she opened her Bible.

This Melchizedec was king of Salem and priest of God Most High. He met Abraham returning from the defeat of the kings and blessed him, and Abraham gave him a tenth of everything. First, the name Melchizedec means "King of righteousness" then also "King of Salem" means "King of peace." Without father or mother, without genealogy, without beginning of days, or end of life, resembling the Son of God, he remains a priest forever. (Hebrews 7:1–3)

After I finished reading, I asked her straight, "Don't you think this great man's arrival or existence was more miraculous than Jesus, who was known to his people since his birth to his ascent to heaven?"

Jesus' miraculous Acts in support of his being equal to God

In reply to my question, the young woman reminded me politely of Jesus' miraculous acts and particularly of his bringing the four-day old dead body of his friend Lazarus out of his grave alive. She read about this stunning miracle from John 11:39-44, and then said, "You must know there is none but God Who can control life and death. If Jesus were not God as you think, then," The young lady asked me, being nice and polite, "How could he bring his four days old dead friend back to life?"

"Let me answer your question," I said to my young friend, "With another act of miracle from the book of Ezekiel, in the Old Testament."

From her apprehensive look, I understood she was not aware of what I was going to read to her.

I opened the book of Ezekiel and read to her first ten verses from the chapter 37.

After I finished reading, I asked her casually: "So, what do you think of him who turned the whole valley of dried-up bones of a large army to stand on their feet, alive?" In her silence, I asked her again, "Don't you think, if the status of God is achieved through one's acts of miracles, then that Prophet's chance of being God or His equal was invariably better than Jesus?"

When she did not answer I continued, "In fact, it is not only Jesus or the other Prophet of God, there were many of them who also stunned their people by the acts of their miracles. As for example, Abraham remained unburned when the Pagan king threw him inside the gulf of fire. Moses made a dry path in the middle of the sea when he touched the water by his stick. Similarly, the trees and the mountains used to sing with David in praise of God and his son Solomon could change the course of air by his command. But none of them was worshiped as God, because they performed those miracles being inspired by God so that people of their time believed them as His messengers and obey His commands that He sent through them for their guidance. Same thing happened to Jesus when God sent him last from the House of Israel for the guidance of his own people. In many places of the Gospel, Jesus admitted it openly and people of his time knew it, too. (John 3:2; 5:19-20; 11:4).

Jesus was worshiped as God by his people

"Yes, Madam, I understand your point," my young friend tried to convince me, "But the Gospel also tells us Jesus was worshiped as God by his people. Don't you think Jesus would have stopped them if he knew he was not God?"

"Jesus did not stop them because he knew it was not that kind of worship which men used to do for their Creator-Lord. People of Jesus' time and specially his disciples were seen to bow down or prostrate before Jesus to kiss his hands or feet as a mark of their excessive love, respect, and allegiance to him. Jesus accepted it in good gesture because it was also a part of their culture at that time.

"You will still find this custom among many other races or religion of the world except in Islam. I mean, except the Muslims, you will find others who bow down and even prostrate themselves before their kings, the heads of the states or their religious organizations. You certainly don't believe their people worship them as God, right?"

The young lady did not answer. Rather, she chose to leave with lots of thanks and appreciations for sharing my thoughts and knowledge with her.

Jesus was not a deity, but a man of flesh and blood

Reverend, I would like to end this letter with the episode of the fig tree, as it is described in the Gospel of Mark. I have some good reason to claim that this is another instance to affirm Jesus was no deity, but a man of flesh and blood. Let me explain why or how after I quote the incident.

(Mark 11:12-16) *The next day as they were leaving Bethany, Jesus was hungry. Seeing in the distance a fig tree in leaf, he went to find out* if it had any fruit. When he reached it, he found nothing but leaves, because was not the season for the figs. Then he said to the tree, May no one ever eat fruit from you again. And his disciples heard him say it.

On reaching Jerusalem, Jesus entered the temple courts and began driving out those who were buying and selling there. He overturned the tables of the money changers and the benches of those selling doves and would not allow anyone to carry merchandise through the temple courts.

(Mark 11:20) In the morning, as they went along, they saw the fig tree withered from the roots.

When I read this passage for the first time, I had a weird feeling about Jesus whom the Muslims love and respect dearly as a mighty messenger of God. I felt weird, because this kind of intolerance, anger, or ill-manner was not expected of him, who has been described in the Quran being noble, chaste, righteous, and close to God. I asked myself in wonder how could a rational, righteous, and a beloved person of God curse a tree for its' failing to provide him with untimely fruits to appease his hunger! Did not his Predecessors suffer a lot more torture and torment, hatred and hostility, pains and persecution while striving for the cause of God?

God has His own unique way to save the truth and to expose it

Then, it suddenly occurred to me that God has His own unique way to save the truth and to expose it. In this small incident, Jesus, who used to say or do everything by the command of God, left many clear indications for his followers to help them reflect and realize why they should not worship him as God in any form or manner. We may now verify those indications one by one.

I already have mentioned before that Jesus was ignorant of the last hour, but now we came to know he was not even aware of the season of the fig. If Jesus were God, God incarnate, or one of the Gods in the Trinity, nothing could escape from his knowledge or vision. But as he was a man of flesh and blood, this kind of ignorance, obliviousness, or forgetfulness was quite expected and understood.

If Jesus were God as his devoted followers claim about him, he would be completely free from all kinds of human needs and weakness like hunger, thirst, fatigue, or frustration, as God really is. But as Jesus was a human being, he felt hungry and became truly angry when he saw no fruit in the tree to appease his hunger. Not only that, it made him so upset and offended that he cursed the fig tree instantly and made it barren forever for no fault of its' own.

Jesus' attitude or his outburst with the common and ordinary salespersons in the temple of Jerusalem was not at all godly. I think, there are many simple and ordinary people in and around us who could have scored more points than Jesus in the test of patience, manners, or self-control.

At this point, I would rather like to believe that Jesus acted like that on purpose and being inspired by God. I have quoted before several verses from the Gospel where Jesus claimed himself that he never said or did anything but by the command of God (John 12: 49-50). I would like to support his claim with another statement in the Gospel.

In Matthew 15:32–36, we have learnt how Jesus fed the multitudes with a few pieces of bread. In the same way, he could have made the tree full of figs instead of making it barren forever with his curse. But he did not, because God wanted to leave this incident as an eye-opener for them who deviated themselves from the eternal truth of His First Commandment and began to worship Him along with Jesus.

Have faith in God. **Jesus answered (Mark 11:22)**

While passing by the fig tree next morning, some of Jesus' disciples drew his attention to the dried-up fig tree. But he ignored it, and said,

Have faith in God. Jesus answered. Truly I tell you, if anyone says to this mountain, Go, throw yourself into the sea, and does not doubt in their heart but believes that what they say will happen, it will be done for them. (Mark 11:22–23)

With this sermon, Jesus appeared again in his true form, the role of a chosen Messenger of God. He sounded exceptionally cool and confident when he started teaching his disciples how to keep their faith in God and what they could achieve through the strength of their unquestioning and unconditional faith in Him. By this statement, Jesus also wanted them to know that turning a live tree to a dry log was nothing in comparison to moving a mountain from its place and throwing it into the sea. But it is also possible if only they could always keep their faith in God intact or uncontaminated under all circumstances.

Jesus left for his followers some precautionary notes as a reminder to them

Along with this instance and advice, Jesus also left for his followers some precautionary notes as a reminder to them especially when the false prophets would come with their invented doctrines to deceive them in his name and to divert them from his teaching. Out of many such statements, I have quoted below only a few of them.

(Matthew 7:15) *Beware of the false prophets, which come to you in sheep's clothing, but inwardly they are ravening wolves.*

(Matthew 24:4–5) *Take heed that no man deceives you. For many shall come in my name, saying, I am Christ; and shall deceive many.*

(Matthew 15:9) *But in vain they do worship me, teaching for doctrines the commandments of men.*

(Matthew 7:21) *Not everyone who says to me, Lord, Lord, will enter the kingdom of heaven, but only the one who does the will of my Father who is in heaven.*

(Matthew 15:13-14) *He replied, every plant that my heavenly Father has not planted will be pulled up by the roots.*

Leave them; they are blind guides. If the blind lead the blind, both will fall into a pit.

(Matthew 5:19) *Therefore anyone who sets aside one of the least of these commands and teaches others accordingly will be called least in the kingdom of heaven but whoever practices and teaches these commands will be called great in the kingdom of heaven.*

(John 14:15) *If you love me, keep my commandments.*

(John 8:32) *If you hold to my teaching, you are really my disciples. Then, you will know the truth, and the truth will set you free.*

Reverend, with those precautionary notes in the Gospel, Jesus also asked his followers to pay heed to his Comforter Muhammad who would come after him along with the Quran, testifying in it clearly who he really was and what he taught them in the name of God for their guidance.

Therefore everyone who hears these words of mine and puts them into practice, is like a wise man who built his house upon on the rock: …But everyone who hears these words of mine, and does not put them into practice is like a foolish man who built his house on sand.
(Matthew 7:24, 26)

Letter 12

Our Only Way to Heaven as Described in both Bible and Quran

The one who sins is the one who will die. The child will not share the guilt of the parent, nor will the parent share the guilt of the child. The righteousness of the righteous will be credited to them, and the wickedness of the wicked will be charged against them.

—Ezekiel 18:20

Reverend,

Early one afternoon on a Labor Day weekend, when I was editing the last and the most complicated topic of my writing about Jesus on a file of my lap which I named "Our only way to heaven," I was revisited by Mrs. Martha Miller whom I mentioned in letter six. From my previous experience with my other missionary friends, I really did not expect her to visit me again so soon. So, you may easily guess how I felt when I opened the door and saw her standing with a beautiful smile right before me? Not only that, with my recent topic of writing in my head, I took her again to be God sent. So naturally, I thanked her cordially for her second visit and welcomed her in cheerfully.

Writing on Jesus without his atonement is like a description of the Sun without its light.

After we sat down face-to-face in the same living room beside the same coffee table overloaded with my books and other stuffs, she said to me with a polite hesitation, "I think, I chose a wrong time to come. I was in the neighborhood and I also had some free time, so I …."

"Mrs. Miller, we are the servants of God, so every time is good time for us." I said to her interrupting. "You may now relax with a glass of cold orange juice and some homemade cookies. Just give me a few moments."

But before I got up, she stopped me pleading, "Please don't. I already overate in my lunch and I have to attend a housewarming party, in the evening, so don't worry." Then she asked me abruptly but politely, "By the way, have you finished your writing on Jesus?"

"O my God! Do you still remember it?" I could not hide my pleasure to hear it from her.

"Shouldn't I? You are writing on Jesus who is dearer to me than my own life. So, tell me," she asked, "Are you still writing? Or have you completed it?"

"No, not yet. I'm now working on Jesus' atonement-the last topic of my writing." I responded her being cautious and careful.

"That's wonderful. It means you are almost done, right?"

"I've no idea. After I finished writing about it, I find it too delicate and sensitive to include in my book. Sometimes I think to drop this topic entirely from my writing."

"Then you are thinking to drop something without which your writing on Jesus will remain incomplete. It will be like a description of the Sun without its light."

From this comment of her, I instantly thought she might help me to find the answers of many unsolved and unavoidable questions that is bothering me since I knew about Jesus' atonement from my other missionary friends and also from the study of both Quan and Bible. So, I asked her, choosing my questions carefully, "Do you mean other sides of Jesus' life become insignificant without his atonement?"

Jesus' true status cannot be measured without his atonement

"Right. We believe Jesus' true status cannot be measured without his atonement. It is, in fact the only thing that separates Jesus from all other prophets of God."

"May I please know how?"

She said, "Jesus' status is different, because he came to give his life for the sin of mankind, while other prophets were sent only for the guidance of their own people."

"Yes, I got your point. But will you please tell me why Jesus needed to give his life for the sin of mankind! Are not men responsible for their own sin?" I asked her to make sure whether she tells me anything new or different from what I already learnt from my other missionary friends.

Man is born with the stain of Adam's sin

To my surprise I heard her repeat the same story that I already knew but couldn't accept because of lack of evidence. Mrs. Miller told me how Adam-the father of mankind disobeyed God by the instigation of the Satan and ate the forbidden fruit from the Garden of Eden. Since breaking the law of God was a sin, Adam became the first sinner and because of him all his children were born with the stain of his sin."

"You mean all of them were born as sinners, without committing any sin?"

"Yes. Saint Augustine has said, *No one is clean, not even if his life be only for a day.*"

"If it is so, as you claim, it must be a very frightening situation for all of us, Right?" I asked her to know the ins and out about the validity of Jesus' atonement for the sin of mankind.

For all have sinned and fall short before the glory of God

"It is indeed", Mrs. Miller began to explain, "Because it is a sin over which we have no control and from which we have no escape. Saint Paul has said in the book of Roman *all have sinned and fall short before the glory of God.*" (Roman 3:23) It means all of us- both righteous and the unrighteous are stained with Adam's sin and became equal before the glory of God and are destined for eternal hell. You may now question," She stopped for a moment and said, "How the righteous be considered sinners and punished in the hell equally with the unrighteous. Right?"

"Yes, I was about to ask you."

"Let me tell you why or how. It is like," She began to clarify, "Putting a drop of vinegar in a cup of fresh milk. The same way, the stain of Adam's sin prevents a man from being completely holy despite of all his good deeds, thus making him unfit to deserve a place in heaven. But, thanks to God for His justice and endless love and mercy for all of mankind, because He loved them so much that He did not want to punish them in hell. Rather, He wanted them to have eternal life in heaven as a free-gift from Him!"

"A free-gift? O my God! I never heard of it before.!" I could not hide my excitement.

"Yes, it is! But we also know that heaven is the abode of God and because of that it is the holiest place of all. It means to deserve a place in heaven we should be purified first from our sin." Mrs. Miller stopped for a moment and then continued, "So, God took a unique measure to cleanse our sin and to make us eligible for heaven. He wanted to purify us with the holy blood of the sinless. Now the question is whose blood could be more holy than the blood of His only begotten and beloved Son Jesus? It was then God sent Jesus to atone for our sin. I hope, now you understand why Jesus' atonement matters to us so much."

While listening to her minutely, I remembered that the word "begotten" from the phrase "His only begotten Son" in the verse 16 of John 3, has now been removed as an unauthorized interpretation from all modern versions of the Bible. But without mentioning it, I said, "As Muslims, we also believe Jesus was holy and sinless, and so was his mother Mary."

"But you do not believe in Jesus' sacrifice for your sin. Right?"

"Right, because," I said to her with a bit hesitation, "The Quran tells us Jesus was raised up to heaven before he was crucified." (4:157-158)

"I find it really interesting!" Mrs. Miller sounded a bit disappointed. "I mean how does the Quran say it when the Bible tells us clearly Jesus was crucified, resurrected from his grave after three days and then God raised him up to heaven!"

"It is the reason I told you first why I find this topic so delicate and sensitive to include it in my book."

"But Madam, it is the question of your salvation. Shouldn't you take it seriously and choose your path that will save you from fire and ensure your eternal life in heaven-the ever-happy kingdom of God?"

"Yes, Mrs. Miller, it is the only reason," I tried to tell her truthfully, "I have started reading the Bible so seriously, because I really want to know what the Bible has said about it. But to admit to you frankly, after I read both parts of the Bible, I have several questions which have been bothering me a lot about Jesus' dying for the sin of mankind. May be, you can help me to find the truth I'm looking for."

"Sure. What do you want to know?" Mrs. Miller looked happy and confident.

"Thanks a lot, Mrs. Miller. But before I begin, I want you to know and remember that many of my questions may sound to you unpleasant or inappropriate, but I need to ask them not to hurt your faith or feeling, but purely for the sake of truth. I hope, you will understand, right?"

"Don't worry. I'll remember and understand." Mrs. Miller assured me with a gracious smile.

"Thanks. Let's begin first with sin, because it is the only reason you believe Jesus' had to give his life."

"Yes. So, what is your question?"

"I like to know first what the Bible has really said about sin."

Sin is breaking the law of God

"The Bible says sin is breaking the law of God, or to do something against the command of God."

> *Everyone who sins breaks the law; in fact sin is lawlessness. (1 John 3:4).*

While listening to her, I also remembered, the Quran also said more or less the same thing about committing a sin.

> *If anyone disobeys God and His messengers, he has indeed strayed clearly in a wrong path. (33:36)*

"My next question is, if sin is breaking the law of God, doesn't it tell us clearly whoever disobeys God, commits a sin and becomes a sinner?"

"Sure. There is no question about that."

If sin is breaking the law of God, how a new-born child becomes a sinner?

"In that case, how could a newborn child become a sinner without committing a sin?"

"I think, I already explained it to you." Mrs. Miller reminded me politely and promptly.

"Yes, you did. But what you said does not match a bit with the definition of sin. It matches more with an incurable and transmittable disease the virus of which may pass forever through the genes of a sick father to his children. Do you think," I asked her seriously, "Adam's sin was a kind of transmittable virus that has contaminated all his progeny, making them sick or sinner until Jesus was sent to atone for them?"

"Yes, you got it right because sin is also a kind of sickness. Man commits sin from the sickness of his heart. Doesn't he?"

"Mostly, but you also know there are other causes, too. But we don't need go into that. I just want to know if we believe man commits sin from the sickness of his heart, then we should also believe God made Adam with a sick heart which was prone to sin. In that case, how could we blame Adam even for his own sin?"

"Sorry, I beg to differ from you." Mrs. Miller said being nice and polite. "God did not make Adam with a sick heart. He gave him intelligence, insight, and freedom of choice to obey His command or to disobey it. But Adam chose to disobey when the devil instigated him to eat the forbidden fruit. We believe," Mrs. Miller affirmed, "It is Adam's greed that led him to obey the Satan and to disobey God."

"But like Adam," I tried to oppose her gently, "All his children were also given intelligence, insight, and freedom of choice to obey God or to disobey Him. In that case, isn't it most expected that God will punish them who are disobedient to Him?"

"But the book of Roman tells us, *as for one man's disobedience, all men were made sinners so, by the obedience of one man, they were made righteous.* (5:19)

I was about to tell her 'It is not the statement of Jesus or any of his true disciples. It is the statement of Paul, who never met Jesus but claimed to learn everything from Jesus through his dream or vision. May I please know what Jesus, or his true disciples have said about it?' But keeping my questions to myself I said, "But the line you just quoted, tells us clearly that men will be righteous by the obedience of one man, it didn't tell us by the blood or the sacrifice of one man, right?"

"It is implied. I already told you that before God has made his only son die for the sin of all men out of His endless mercy and love for them. In other word, the purpose of God has been served through His only son's sacrifice which he made because of his absolute obedience to his Father."

"Does it mean God took Adam's sin as an excuse so that He could use it later to prove His endless love for all of mankind, and to prove His only son's absolute obedience to Him?"

"Sorry, it is not an excuse," Mrs. Miller sounded a bit offended. "It is an instance. We believe God is most kind, just, fair and forgiving. He wanted to show His love and favors to all of us equally by forgiving our sins and assuring for us a happy eternal life in heaven. We also believe," Mrs. Miller affirmed, "God's love and justice to all of mankind has been expressed fully through giving His only son die for them."

"Does it mean I am now free from all my sins by Jesus' holy blood and I shall now go to heaven straight after I die?"

"Sure, if you only believe in Jesus as your only Savior, and he gave his life for your sin."

"May I please know why? Didn't you just say God made His only Son die for the sin of all of mankind to show His endless love and justice for them? In that case, shouldn't we expect Jesus' holy blood purified us all from our sin the moment it was shed for us!"

"Yes, of course!" she agreed, "But God also wanted us all to show our sincere love, gratitude, and obedience to Jesus for what he did for us. I mean, how could we expect a sin free eternal life, if we don't believe in his unconditional love and sacrifice for us, or deny it?"

A few pertinent questions with no acceptable answer

"Yes, you have a point there. Despite of that, I like to know," I asked her politely, "What do you think of those infants in the Christian family who have died without knowing anything about their inborn sin or about

Jesus' sacrifice for their sin?"

"Since they were born and died as Christians, we believe they will be saved through the faith of their parents."

"If so, what do you think of them who lived and died with their inborn sin before the arrival of Jesus?"

"I think we should leave the matter to God. He would certainly take care of them."

In reply to that, I remained silent for a while and then asked her again being cautious and careful, "Then, why God sent so many messengers before Jesus, telling their people constantly and consistently to strive for their eternal life through keeping His commands, if He knew all along nothing could purify them but the holy blood of His only Son Jesus?"

"I already told you before that God sent those prophets only for the guidance of their own people. But after the arrival of Jesus as the Savior of mankind, everything has changed. Now, we need to seek for our eternal life only through having faith in Jesus as our only Savior and in his dying for us."

'If it is so, then why God sent again Prophet Muhammad with the same eternal truth of His First Commandment that Jesus preached and practiced himself all through his life as did all his predecessors before him?'

I was about to ask her, but I did not. I felt it was not easy to discard anything to be wrong or false which people had believed and still believe to be true for hundreds of years. In this interesting and amazing situation, I had no other alternative but to check the validity of Jesus' atonement as we find it in the narration of both Bible and Quran. From my past experience with my other missionary friends, I knew very well they had lots of reservation about the teaching of the Quran that God sent to Prophet Muhammad as His last and final Guidebook for all of mankind. Despite of that, I needed to quote from both parts of the Bible and also from the Quran only to establish my point that our only way to redeem our sin and to have our eternal life in heaven, has remained the same in the Gospel of Jesus, in the Torah which God sent to Moses about thirteen hundred years before the arrival of Jesus and also in the Quran that Muhammad received from God nearly six hundred years after Jesus' ascent to heaven.

All the scriptures tell us to repent for our sin and to strive for our eternal life through keeping the commands of God.

But keeping my thoughts to myself, I said to her frankly, "Mrs. Miller, I heard what you said about Jesus and why he had to give his life. Will you mind, if we try to know what our Holy Scriptures-both Bible and Quran have really said about it?"

"Sure. I'd love to know." Mrs. Miller seemed to me genuinely curious and it made me feel happy and relaxed.

"Thanks. Please give me a moment. I need to go to the file in my lap where I stored every piece of information since I intended to write about it."

"Sure. Take your time."

"Thanks." My laptop was already in sleep mode, so it took me no longer than few seconds to open my file which I named "Our Only Way to heaven."

"Mrs. Miller, since you believe," I said to her while browsing on my file, "Jesus had to give his life for the sin of Adam, we shall check first what the Old Testament and the Quran have really said about it. Then we shall examine what the Gospel of Jesus has said about our sin and and how to get rid of it. I think this comparative study might help us to find the answer we are looking for, right?"

"Yes, I hope so." Mrs. Miller agreed holding a graceful smile on her beautiful face.

The Old Testament tells us man is accountable for what he does

I stopped browsing when I found the chapter on Adam and Eve. Then I said, "Here it is. Mrs. Miller. The incident of Adam and Eve has been mentioned in the second and third chapter in Genesis-the first Book of the Old Testament. I hope, you know what happened to them when they ate the forbidden fruit by the instigation of the Satan, right?"

"Yes, it is known to all."

"Right. The Book of Genesis tells us God made both the instigator and the instigated equally responsible for what they did and expelled them all from heaven dictating the nature of their punishment separately. But nowhere in the Old Testament, Adam was blamed for the sin of mankind.

Rather, I came across with many statements where we have been told clearly man is responsible for what he does, and no one can be held responsible for the sin of others. I would read to you a few of them that I have saved on my file. You may check in your Bible when I read them mentioning the name of the Book along with the number of the chapter and the verses."

"I don't have to check. I know very well you will not misquote."

"Thanks a lot for your faith in me." Then I began to read those verses from the screen of my lap as clearly as possible.

(Deuteronomy 24:16) *Parents are not to be put to death for their children, nor children be put to death for their parents; each will die for their own sin.*

(Ezekiel 18:20) *The one who sins is the one who will die. The child will not share the guilt of the parent, nor will the parent share the guilt of the child. The righteousness of the righteous will be credited to them, and the wickedness of the wicked will be charged against them.*

(Ezekiel 18:26–27) *If a righteous person turns from their righteousness and commits sin, they will die for it; because of the sin they have committed they will die. But if a wicked person turns away from the wickedness they have committed and does what is just and right, they will save their life.*

(Proverbs 11:5) *The righteousness of the perfect shall direct his way: but the wicked shall fall by his own wickedness.*

After I finished reading, I said to her, "Mrs. Miller, we shall now check what the Quran has said about our sin."

"Please go ahead, I'm listening"

The Quran also tells us man is accountable for his own deeds

"Thanks." Then I continued, "You will find the story of Adam and Eve has been told and retold in many places of the Quran. (2:30-39; 7:19-25; 20:116-124) The Quran also tells us Adam and Eve disobeyed God and ate the forbidden fruit by the instigation of the Satan. Then as a punishment to their disobedience, they were also expelled from heaven along with the Satan as their open enemy. But nowhere in the Quran Adam was held responsible for the sin of his children. Not only that, like the Old Testament of the Bible, the Quran also tells us repeatedly man is accountable for his own deeds and no one will bear the burden of others. Let me read to you some of them." Then I began to read from the file of my lap.

(2:141) *That is a nation who has already passed. They are responsible for what they did, and you are responsible for what you do, you shall not be questioned about their deeds.*

(17:15) *He that seeks guidance shall be guided to his own advantage, but he that goes astray does so to his own loss. No bearer shall bear the burden of another on the Day of Judgment.*

(29:69) *As for those who strive for Our Cause, We will surely guide them to Our Ways; rest assured that Allah is with the righteous.*

(31:33) *O mankind! Fear of your Lord and fear that Day when no father shall avail his son nor a son his father.*

(40:58) *Not equal are the blind and those who see clearly: nor are those who believe and work deeds of righteousness and those who do evil. Little do you reflect!*

I raised my head from my lap and said, "Mrs. Miller, you must have noticed the bottom line of all those statements from both the Old Testament and the Quran, is one and the same. It is man is accountable for his own deeds and no one will bear the burden of others. In other word, the righteous and the unrighteous are not the same in the eyes of God. Right?"

"Let me reserve all my comments until you come to the Gospel of Jesus."

"As you please. Then without wasting our time, we may now check what the Old Testament tells us to do to redeem our sin."

The Old Testament tells us repentance is required for the remission of sin

"There are many verses in the Old Testament where we have been told clearly sincere repentance is required for the remission of our sin. Out of many such verses, let me read to you only a few of them."

(2 Chronicles 7:14) *If my people, who are called by my name, will humble themselves and pray and seek my face, and turn from their wicked ways, then I will hear from heaven, and I will forgive their sin, and will heal their land.*

(Isaiah 55:7) *Let the wicked forsake their ways and the unrighteous man his thoughts: and let him return unto the Lord, and he will have mercy upon him; and to our God, for he will abundantly pardon.*

(Ezekiel 18:21) *But if a wicked person turns away from all the sins they have committed and keeps all my decrees and does what is just and right, that person will surely live; they will not die.*

(Ezekiel 18:30) *Therefore, you Israelites, I will judge each of you according to your own ways, declares the Sovereign LORD. Repent! Turn away from all your offences; then sin will not be your downfall.*

(Psalm 37:28–29) *Turn from the evil and do good; then you will dwell in the land forever. For the Lord loves the just and will not forsake his faithful ones.*

"Mrs. Miller," I said after I finished reading from different parts of the Old Testament, "Please listen what the Quran tells us to do for the remission of our sin."

The Quran also tells us repentance is required for the remission of sin

"You may feel surprised to know, the Quran also tells us repentance is required for the remission of our sin. Out of many such verses, I shall read to you only a few of them. Then I began to read from the file of my lamp.

(4:110) *If anyone does evil or wrongs his own soul but afterwards seeks Allah's forgiveness, he will find Allah Oft-Forgiving, Most Merciful.*

(11:3) *Seek the forgiveness of your Lord and turn to Him in repentance.*

(16:119) *Your Lord is indeed Forgiving and Merciful to those who do something wrong through ignorance, but later repent and rectify their ways.*

(17:25) *Your Lord knows best what is in your hearts. If you do good deeds, certainly He is most forgiving to those who turn to Him again and again in true repentance.*

(20:82) *But the one who repents, becomes a believer, does good deeds and follows the Right Way, shall be forgiven.*

(39:53–55) *O My slaves who have transgressed against their souls, do not despair of Allah's mercy, for Allah forgives all sins. Truly, He is the Oft-Forgiving, the Most Merciful. Turn in repentance to your Lord and submit to Him before the torment comes upon you when you will find none to help you.*

"Mrs. Miller, I hope you have seen both the Old Testament and the

Quran tell us to do the same thing to redeem our sin. It is to repent for our sin sincerely and to rectify our way through keeping the commands of God. Right?"

"Right." Mrs. Miller responded in brief.

Quran says Adam and Eve repented for their being disobedient to God

As Mrs. Miller told me she would reserve her comment until I come to the Gospel of Jesus, I availed the chance and wanted to share with her an incident related to Adam's sin that I did not mention to her before. So, I said: "You may feel surprised to know the Quran also tells us that repentance for sin began when Adam and Eve deviated first from the command of God. They became truly repentant after they ate the forbidden fruit by the instigation of the Satan. As it was their first mistake, they did not know what to do with their feeling of guilt. It was then God Who knew perfectly well about the intention of their heart, inspired them how to ask for His mercy and forgiveness in that kind of slip or fall from His commands. Thus, being inspired by God, they said to Him pleading, *Our Lord! We have wronged our own souls: If you do not forgive us and bestow your mercy upon us, we shall certainly be the losers.* (7:23)

"From the description of the Quran, we also have learnt God accepted their repentance and forgave them totally before they were sent down to earth. At this point, I also like to mention that Muslims all over the world also invoke the same prayer to God for His mercy and forgiveness as did Adam and Eve in the Garden of Eden."

"It is really impressive!" Mrs. Miller said in appreciation.

God's guidance for mankind began with Adam and Eve in the Garden of Eden

"Yes, it is. In this connection, I also want you to know that like repentance for sin, God's guidance for mankind also began with Adam and Eve before they were sent down to earth along with the Satan as their open enemy. The Quran tells us after they were forgiven, God sent them to earth along with His guidance. "Let me read to you what God said to them," I said to her while browsing on my file. Then I began to read after I found it:

"Get down from here all of you [Adam, Eve, and Satan]; Henceforth there shall come to you guidance from Me, and those who accept and follow it shall have nothing to fear or to regret. But those who reject and defy our revealed guidance will be inmates of hellfire, where they shall live forever." (2:38–39

"In another place of the Quran God says to the Satan directly: *Get out from here (heaven) disgraced and and expelled. Surely, I will fill the hell with you and whoever of mankind will follow you."* (7:18)

"Mrs. Miller, according to that promise of God, we believe the heritage of prophethood and the legacy of revelation that began with Adam-the Father of mankind, finally ended with Muhammad-the last and the final Prophet of God. But the bottom line in the guidance of God that He revealed through all His messengers beginning from Adam to Muhammad has always remained the same or unchanged. It is, whoever follows the guidance of God, will have eternal life in heaven and whoever follows the Satan and deviates from His guidance, will be punished in hell. Mrs. Miller," I said while taking my cursor down, "Both Old Testament and the Quran have numerous verses where God has said to His people clearly what they needed to do to have their eternal life in heaven or what they should not do to save them from the fire of hell. But to save our time, I would only read a few of them from the Old Testament and then from the Quran."

Instances from the Old Testament

"In different places of the Old Testament, Moses-the mighty Messenger from the House of Israel, is seen to ask his people to obey the commands of God for their eternal life in heaven. Let me read to you some of them. Then I read:

Hear O Israel, and be careful to obey so that it may go well with you and that ye may increase greatly in a land flowing with milk and honey, just as the LORD, the God of your ancestors, promised you.

Hear, O Israel: The Lord our God is one Lord. Love the LORD your God with all your heart and with all your soul and with all your strength. (Deuteronomy 6:3–5)

: Fear the LORD your God, serve him only and take your oath in his name. Do not follow other gods, the gods of the people around you. (Deuteronomy 6:13–14)

: *Honor your father and your mother - You shall not murder. You shall not commit adultery. You shall not steal. You shall not give false testimony against your neighbor. You shall not covet your neighbor's house. You shall not covet your neighbor's wife...* (Exodus 20:12–17)

After I finished reading, I said, "Mrs. Miller, we shall now check in the Quran to see what God has commanded us to do to return to Him in heaven, and what He forbade us doing to save us from the fire of hell." Then I read to her the following verses of the Quran from the screen of my lap.

Instances from the Quran

:[O Muhammad], *tell them: I am but a human being like you; the revelation is sent to me to proclaim that your God is One God; therefore, whoever hopes to meet his Lord, let him do good deeds and join no other deity in the worship of his Lord.* (18:110)

:*Your Lord has decreed to you that: You shall worship none but Him, and you shall be kind to your parents; if one or both of them attain their old age in your lifetime, you shall not say to them any word of contempt nor repel them and you shall address them in kind words.* (17:23)

:*O believers! Stand firm for justice and bear true witness for the sake of Allah, even though it goes against yourselves, your parents, or your relatives. ... If you distort your testimony or decline to give it, then you should remember that Allah is fully aware of your actions.* (4:135)

:*You shall not commit adultery; surely it is a shameful deed and an evil way. You shall not kill anyone whom Allah has forbidden, except for just cause.* (17:32–33)

...*those who commit evil and become encircled in sin are the inmates of Hellfire. As for those who believe in God and do good deeds, they will be the residents of Paradise.* (2:81–82)

"Mrs. Miller", I looked up from my laptop, and said, " I read those statements from both Old Testament and the Quran only to show you the consistency in the guidance of God regarding the sin of man and what we need to do to redeem our sin, to return to God in the eternal heaven and to save us from the fire of hell. In other word, our way to heaven or to save us from the fire of hell, has remained the same in the teaching of both Old Testament and the Quran. Both the scriptures tell us to worship none but

One God, to repent for our sin, and to strive for our eternal life through keeping His commands. Right?"

"But I also told you," Mrs. Miller broke her long silence, "That everything has changed since Jesus was sent as the Savior of mankind."

Our way to heaven has also remained unchanged in the teaching of Jesus

"Yes, I remember. But while reading the Gospel," I told her being cautious and careful, "I came across many of its statements where Jesus admitted himself clearly that he was sent not to destroy the laws of God or His prophets, but to fulfill them. He also asked his people not to break any of the laws but to compete for their eternal life through keeping the commands of God. I hope you will understand my point much better if I read to you some verses from the Gospel-the Book you believe yourself as a true account of Jesus' own words and deeds." Then I began to read to her the following verses from the file of my lap.

(Mark 12:29–30) *The first of all the commandments is, hear, O Israel: the Lord our God is one Lord: and thou shalt love the Lord thy God with all thy heart, and with all thy soul, and with all thy mind, and with all thy strength: this is the first commandment.*

(Matthew 4:10) *Get thee hence, Satan: for it is written, thou shalt worship the Lord thy God, and Him only shalt thou serve.*

(Matthew 5:17–20) *Do not think that I have come to abolish the law or the prophets; I have not come to abolish them but to fulfill them. For truly I tell you, until heaven and earth disappear, not the smallest letter, nor the least stroke of a pen, will by any means disappear from the law until everything is accomplished. Therefore, anyone who sets aside one of the least of these commands and teaches others accordingly will be called least in the kingdom of heaven, but whoever practices and teaches these commands will be called great in the kingdom of heaven. For I tell you that unless your righteousness surpasses that of the Pharisees and the teachers of the law, you will certainly not enter the kingdom of heaven.*

(Matthew 19:16–17) *Behold, one came and said unto him* [Jesus] *Good*

Master, what good thing shall I do, that I may have eternal life?

And he said unto him, Why callest thou me good?

There is none good but one, that is, God: but if thou wilt enter into life, keep the commandments.

After I finished reading, I said, "Mrs. Miller, you must have noticed Jesus also asked his people to strive for their eternal life through keeping the commands of God as did all his predecessors before him and as did Muhammad who was sent after him. Will you please," I asked, "Why Jesus taught them so, if he really knew all men were born sinners because of Adam, and nothing could purify them or make them eligible for heaven except his holy blood?"

Mrs. Miller looked a bit hesitant at my question. So, I told her again, "Let me draw your attention to another statement of Jesus from the Gospel of Mark 10 before you answer my question. The number of the verses is 14 and 15."

Jesus says heaven is meant for the children

Then I read to her from the file of my lap.

: When Jesus saw this, (his disciples to rebuke the people for bringing their children to him for his blessing) he was indignant. He said to them, Let the children come to me, and do not hinder them, for the kingdom of God belongs to such as these. Truly I tell you, anyone who will not receive the kingdom of God like a little child will never enter it.

"Mrs. Miller," I asked her after I read, "If a man is born with the stain of Adam's sin and Jesus' holy blood is required to purify them, then why Jesus tells his disciples heaven is meant for the children? Doesn't it tell us indirectly but undoubtedly that Jesus was not aware of men's inborn sin? In that case, why would he atone for the sin that he was not even aware of?"

God says or acts many ways the mystery of which is beyond our comprehension

Mrs. Miller remained silent for a moment and then said, "Sorry, I have no answer for that, except telling you that God says or acts many ways, the mystery of which is beyond our comprehension."

The same old answer that my missionary friends used to give when they failed to provide any acceptable explanation for Jesus' atonement. But I really did not expect to hear it from an enlightened and educated teacher like her. I understood once again that our faith in God, whether it is blind or prudent, is equally strong and unshakable. So, keeping my frustration to myself, I said to her very politely and choosing my words carefully, "Yes, I agree. Our intelligence is too short to comprehend the mystery in the words or in the acts of God. But Mrs. Miller, we are not talking here about the creation of the heavens or earth. Or how God made those celestial bodies to rotate around their orbits without making them fall or crash into one other? We are simply trying to know our way to heaven from the scriptures of God and in the teaching of all His messengers. In that case, wouldn't we expect His path to be plain, simple and easy to follow by all human beings without any confusion?"

"Sure, it is what God finally did for all of mankind," Mrs. Miller responded promptly, "I mean what could be easier and simpler than going to heaven only through having faith in Jesus' dying for our sin?"

The way she said, I felt a little nervous, but soon I overcame it. I remembered very well the Gospel had no clear evidence in support of the Original Sin or Jesus' atonement for it, or about his resurrection. So, I did not hesitate to tell her, "Yes, I also believe myself nothing could be easier than that. But to admit frankly, I did not find any clear evidence in the Gospel in support of Jesus' atonement.

"What do you mean?"

"I mean," I tried to collect my strength and then said, "While reading the Gospel, I didn't find any valid evidence to believe Jesus gave his life for the sin of mankind."

"It is not true." Mrs. Miller said curtly after a moment of stunning silence, "The Gospel has clear and valid evidence for it, and it might have escaped your notice!"

"It is quite possible. Would you please read some of them so that I could know the truth and correct my mistake?"

"Sure," Mrs. Miller picked up her Bible from the side table and said, "You'll find it in verse 28 in Matthew 20."

"Thanks."

Jesus came to give his life a ransom for many

When I opened the pages of my copy, I felt relaxed because I read that verse several times since I began to prepare myself to write about Jesus' atonement. Despite of that, I tried to listen to her carefully, when Mrs. Miller began to read slowly and softly in her sweet well-modulated voice

Just as the Son of Man did not come to be served, but to serve, and to give his life as a ransom for many (Matthew 20:28).

After she finished reading, she said, "I hope, now you know why we believe in Jesus' atonement, right?"

"Not completely," I replied, "Can you please tell me why Jesus said he came to give his life for many, instead of saying for the entire mankind?"

After a moment of hesitant silence, Mrs. Miller said, "Jesus said so, because he knew very well that he was sent to give his life for all of mankind, but many of them would deny him as their Savior."

"In that case, may I please know what makes you claim him as the Savior of the entire mankind?"

"We claim so because that is the only reason Jesus was sent for. I mean, the cause or the purpose of his sacrifice remained the same, though others rejected him as their Savior."

While listening to her, I remembered certain statements of Jesus where he spelled out clearly who he really was and why he was sent for. So, I said, "Please let me answer your question with another statement in the Gospel. You will find it in Matthew 15, and the number of the verses is from 22 to 28."

Then I began to read from the file of my lap when Mrs. Miller opened her Bible.

A Canaanite woman from that vicinity came to him crying out, "Lord, son of David, have mercy on me! my daughter is demon-possessed and suffering terribly."

Jesus did not answer a word. So, his disciples came to him and urged him, "Send her away, for she keeps crying out after us."

He answered, "I was sent only for the lost sheep of Israel."

The woman came and knelt before him, "Lord, help me!" She said.

He replied, "It is not right to take the children's bread and toss it to the dogs."

"Yes, it is Lord." She said. "Even the dogs eat the crumbs that fall down from their master's table."

Then Jesus said to her, "Woman, you have great faith! Your request is granted." And her daughter was healed at that moment. (Matthew 15: 22-28)

Jesus refused to cure a sick girl for her non-Jewish affiliation

"Mrs. Miller," I said after I finished reading, "I don't think any explanation is required to understand Jesus' role and mission and how he tried to stick to his assigned job. I hope, you will not mind if I want to know, Jesus who refused to cure a sick girl because of her non-Jewish origin, then how could we expect him to give his life for the sin of all people having so many different races, religions, colors or customs!"

A few moments passed by in silence. Then Mrs. Miller responded with a bit frustration, "But how could we believe otherwise, when the Gospel tells us Jesus gave his life for the sin of all?"

"Okay, we shall come to that after we check Jesus' another statement in the Gospel. You will find it in Matthew 9:13." Then I read to her from the file of my lap,

But go ye and learn what that meaneth, I will have mercy, and not sacrifice: for I am not come to call the righteous, but sinners to repentance.

Jesus was sent to call the sinners to repentance

Then looking at her gentle and impassionate face I said, "Mrs. Miller, I already have quoted a series of verses from both Old Testament and the Quran where we have been told clearly the sinners and the righteous are not equal in the eyes of God. We also learnt sincere repentance is required for the remission of sin. Don't you think Jesus also meant the same when he said he did not come to call the righteous, but the sinners to repent for their sin?"

In her silence I continued, "In other places of the Gospel Jesus is also seen to caution his disciples that they would surely perish if they don't repent. (Luke 13:3, 5) Can you please tell me why Jesus gave so much importance to repentance, if he knew nothing could purify a man from his sin except his holy blood? My other question is, why God Who chose mercy over sacrifice, let His only begotten son die on the Cross for the sin of all when He could forgive them all Himself and send them to heaven?"

"Yes," This time Mrs. Miller came with prompt answer, "God certainly could do it, but He didn't. And we never question God about any of His plans or actions. We believe in Jesus' atonement only because we are told so in the Bible-the Book we believe contains the words of God."

From her prompt reply I understood she did not remember anything that I described to her from both parts of the Holy Bible which she believes to contain the words of God.

It was then, I felt really frustrated, but thinking again of my true intention behind this talk, I tried to overcome my frustration and said to her being cautious and polite, "Mrs. Miller, I appreciate your faith in God and in His words in the Bible. But what would you say if I tell you the Gospel bears numerous instances to prove Jesus didn't die on the Cross?"

"O my God! Do you mean we have believed in something for the last two thousand years that never happened?" Her soft and sweet voice faltered a bit at the end, and I wished I never chose this subject for discussion. But since I did, I felt, I had no point to return, but to proceed.

So, I said, "Mrs. Miller, do you think a wrong thing turns to be right if it is believed to be right for thousands of years? Just remember what our forefathers used to think about the shape of earth only a few centuries ago! But now we have plenty of evidence to …."

"Sorry, I don't think this instance has got anything to do with Jesus' atonement, because we came to know about it from the same Gospel that we have been reading for the last two thousand years." Mrs. Miller cut me off before I finished.

"In that case, we should believe Jesus' early followers, the Nazarenes, had a different Gospel from yours."

"What do you mean?"

"I mean there are many old and authentic books which tell us Jesus' early followers did not believe he died on the cross. But I don't need to go into that controversy. I will try to prove it with the same Gospel that you have been reading and teaching for the last two thousand years."

"You must be crazy," she scoffed. "Do you think anybody would believe that?"

"It is entirely up to them whether they believe it or not. But you have your Holy Bible right before you. If you find me misquote or misinterpret anything about this most important and essential element of your faith, you can stop me right there and I will have a chance to know my mistake and to correct it. So, what do you think? Do you want me to proceed?"

"Sure." To my surprise, Mrs. Miller seemed to be curious to know.

"Thanks. I hope you will stay with me until the end of our discussion." I wanted to make sure so that she would not leave with some excuses in the middle of our discussion, as it happened before many a time with my other missionary friends.

Mrs. Miller looked at her wristwatch and then said, "It is now three fifteen and I've to attend my party at seven. It means, it is okay if I leave by six. You certainly don't need that long to convince me Jesus did not die on the Cross, Right?" She asked me smiling but it did not brighten her face that much as I noticed before.

"Mrs. Miller," I said to her apologetically, "I hope you'll forgive me, if I hurt your faith or feeling anyway. Though I know, I won't say anything to you besides the description of the Gospel."

"Then you don't have to worry, I'm old and matured enough to accept the truth, if I know I am wrong." She responded me curtly.

Jesus was put on the Cross by the Jewish High priest on a false charge of sedition

"Thanks. Let's begin with what caused Jesus to face his death on the Cross. I think, as a devoted Christian and a frequent reader of the Gospel, you know very well Jesus was put on the Cross on a false charge of sedition made by the Jewish High priests and the elders of his own community. They made this conspiracy against him, because they deviated from the Laws of the Torah and became involved with the Romans-the people of the ruling class only for the sake of their personal gain. Not only that they also began to use the laws of the scripture to suit their own purpose. At this stage, when Jesus arrived, fulfilling their dream of the promised Messiah and also confirming the Laws of Moses, they felt themselves threatened and feared losing their place or position that they had been enjoying so long in their community. And, because of that, they had the audacity to deny Jesus as the promised Messiah of God, to misinterpret his teaching, to accuse him with the grave sin of blaspheme and finally to put him on the Cross by framing him in a false charge of sedition.

"The Gospel also tells us," I continued, "That Jesus was betrayed by Judas, one of his close companions, and was handed over to the High priest for thirty pieces of silver. Then he made Jesus arrested by the soldiers of Pilate- the Roman governor in Judaea. Pilate found him innocent and wanted to release him. But he could not, because when the High priest and their misguided followers heard of it, they began to shout for his crucifixion. To pacify the turbulent mob, Pilate delivered Jesus to his soldiers to carry out his persecution. But before they put him on the Cross, they began to humiliate, taunt and torture him in the most cruel and disgraceful manner. Now I would like to know why Jesus let himself be arrested, tortured, and humiliated on a false charge, if he knew he was sent to give his life for the sin of mankind?"

Jesus endured all their taunts and torments in silence to show his love and obedience to God

"There is obviously a good reason for that." Mrs. Miller began to explain. "Jesus knew all along that his blood was required to cleanse the sin of man and he also knew the prophecies made about him in the previous Scriptures would come true. So, he endured all their taunts and tortures in silence only to show his love and obedience to God. Since you read the Gospel so well, you must remember what Jesus did, when the people of the High priest came to arrest him. He commanded one of his men to hold his sword which he raised to strike them. He also mentioned to his disciples that he could pray to God to save him with the help of His angels, but he did not. Because Jesus wanted his people to know and believe that all his sufferings and sacrifices were meant to purify their sin and to ensure their place in heaven which God wanted to accomplish through him. So, it does not matter to us at all how Jesus gave up his life. We simply know and believe he gave his life for us."

Jesus had no intention to give his life on the Cross

"Please don't mind if I tell you there many statements in the Gospel where Jesus made it clear to all that he had no intention to give his life on the Cross."

"That sounds really funny. First, you said Jesus did not die on the Cross, and now you are telling me he had no intention to die?"

"Mrs. Miller, who am I to tell you that? I only want you to know about Jesus' intention that he expressed himself before he was put on the Cross. I hope you will understand my point better if I read to you Jesus' prayers to God when he found his death on the Cross was imminent. You will find it in Matthew 26 and the number is 39 and 42." Then I read to her from the file of my lap.

"My Father, if it is possible, may this cup be taken from me: Yet not as I will, but as you will." He went away a second time, and prayed, "My Father, if it is not possible for this cup to be taken away unless I drink it, may your will be done."

After I finished reading, I asked, "Mrs. Miller, do you think the verses I just read to you, bear any indication of Jesus' willingness to die? The answer is obviously no. Right?"

Mrs. Miller remained silent.

"If you read those verses again carefully, you will find Jesus first wanted to avoid his painful death like an ordinary human being. Then he became ready to accept what God had intended for him like His most obedient servant. But when you read the verse 46 in Matthew 27, you will find him to lose his control at the last moment and to ask God grieving why He had forsaken him. Do you think," I asked, "Jesus would ever make that grievance to God, if he knew he was sent to give his life for the sin of mankind?"

Mrs. Miller looked sad and did not answer.

Jesus did not want to die for a wrong cause

"Mrs. Miller, Jesus made that grievances to God, because he did not want to die for a wrong cause."

"What do you mean by a wrong cause?" Mrs. Miller sounded a bit tensed.

"I already told you that Jesus was put on the Cross on a false charge of sedition made by his own people. So, he had every right to save his life from this kind of disgraceful death. But we should never doubt for a moment that Jesus would hesitate to die, if he knew for sure his blood was required to purify men from their sin and to secure their place in heaven. Didn't he tell his disciples," I tried to remind her, *Greater love has no one than this to lay down one's life for one's friend.* (John 5:13) If Jesus believed a man could prove his love for his friend by giving his life for his sake, then what could he do himself if he really knew his life or blood had anything to do in making all of mankind free from their sin or taking them to heaven. He could certainly give his life happily and without any question. Is not the history of mankind full of noble sacrifices made by the most common and ordinary people for the sake of their country, people, or freedom? So, we have no reason to think Jesus' place or position became any less or low because he did not want to die as a victim of an evil conspiracy. I hope you understand what I mean by it. Right?"

"Yes, I'm trying to understand. Now, tell me please what makes you think Jesus did not die on the Cross?" Mrs. Miller looked serious and concerned.

Circumstantial evidence to prove Jesus did not die on the Cross

"I think so because the Gospel tells us about a series of occurrences that took place from the time of Jesus' crucifixion to his burial and then his coming out from the grave alive. You may of course correct me, if I say something which you do not find in the narration of any of the four Gospels."

"Sure."

"The Gospel tells us Jesus was crucified in the afternoon before the day of the Sabbath. As the Jews were not allowed to do any work on the day of the Sabbath, the Jewish leaders asked Pilate to have the legs of the crucified persons broken and their bodies taken down from the Cross. Accordingly, two soldiers started breaking the legs of other convicts before they approached Jesus. When they came to Jesus, they thought him to be already dead, so they did not break his legs. But when one of the soldiers pierced Jesus' side with his spear, blood and water came out rushing from the wound. It tells us Jesus' body was warm until then, and the circulation of his blood did not stop.

"Then a centurion who saw Jesus to give up his spirit with a loud cry, did not know for certain whether he had died or was unconscious. Same thing happened with Jesus' mother and other two women who stood afar, watching his Crucifixion. They did not know either whether Jesus died or remained unconscious after he was brought down from the Cross.

"We also came to know that two of the convicts who were crucified along with Jesus remained alive when Jesus was thought to be dead.

"Pilate was surprised to hear that Jesus was already dead when Joseph a rich man who became his disciple secretly, approached the governor to take his body for burial. Pilate was surprised because he knew man nailed on the Cross takes time to die.

"The Gospel also tells us that Nicodemus, an influential man in the Jewish community and also a devoted follower of Jesus, accompanied Joseph with a mixture of spices to put on Jesus' body and a piece of linen to cover him following the custom in Jewish burial. They also did not examine Jesus to see whether he was dead or unconscious before they buried him in a newly made tomb close to the place of the crucifixion."

"Do you want me to believe they buried him alive?" asked Mrs. Miller, breaking her long silence

"Mrs. Miller, I am not asking you to believe or to disbelieve anything. I only want you to ponder over the circumstantial evidence where you may find many potential elements to think Jesus did not die on the cross and he was also buried alive. Let me remind you first of the time and situation when Jesus was accused, arrested, humiliated, and put on the Cross.

"Second, think of Jesus' close disciples, who forsook him and fled from him to save their own lives from the assault of his hostile persecutors.

"Third, try to visualize the whole scenario of his crucifixion followed by earthquake, eclipse and total darkness along with other unusual and unexpected freaks of nature. And, above all the next day was the day of Sabbath. So, Jesus was buried in haste by two of his grieved and scared disciples in fear of being seen or caught by his conspirators. Taking all these elements or signs into consideration, I think it is quite human, if the question of examining his body escaped from their minds completely before they buried him in a newly made tomb. You may know it or not, but this kind of mistake still happens today in many places of this modern world. "

Mrs. Miller opened her water-bottle and began to sip in silence.

"The Gospel also tells us about two women who took a mixture of spices and went to Jesus' tomb in the early morning after the day of the Sabbath to anoint his body. They took the mixture, because they somehow believed Jesus was alive or they expected to see him alive. Otherwise, they would not take the trouble of buying the spices and grinding them into a mixture. Do you think Jewish people go inside the tomb to anoint the body of the dead? Obviously not, right?"

Mrs. Miller remained silent.

"From the narration of the Gospel we also came to know two women became stunned with shock and surprise when they found the heavy stone was already removed from the entrance of the tomb and it was empty inside. When they began to look for his body, two angels in dazzling apparel appeared to them and asked, *Why do you look for the living among the dead?* (Luke 24:5)

"Mrs. Miller, the presence of the angels by Jesus' tomb and their question to the women, tells us clearly they knew Jesus was alive inside his tomb. The Gospel also tells us it was the Angel of God who removed the large stone from the entrance of Jesus' tomb so that he could breathe easily and regain his strength and spirit."

I stopped here to take some water to wet my dry lip and tongue.

"You explained it well," Mrs. Miller said casually, "But it is still an assumption. I mean what you said about the possibility of Jesus' survival may be true, but you can't prove it with a hundred percent guarantee that Jesus remained alive after his crucifixion and he was also buried alive."

"You are right," I admitted frankly, "I am unable to do that. May be, it is the reason God Who is Almighty and All-knowing took care of that Himself. Let me tell you what happened after Jesus came out from his tomb."

Resurrection and rising from the dead are not the same

"First, I'd ask you to focus on Jesus' appearance to Mary Magdalene after he came out from his grave. It was dawn and nothing is seen clearly when Mary saw him covered with the cloth of his shroud. She mistook him for a gardener, but she recognized him at once when he called her by her name. Out of her excessive joy and excitement Mary wanted to hug him, but Jesus told her not to touch him. He told her so because she could unknowingly hurt his wounds which were not yet fully healed. Then Jesus asked her to go to his disciples immediately and to tell them that he was about to ascend to his Father in heaven. (John 20:17). By the way, Mrs. Miller," I asked her, "Do you know how Jesus ascended to heaven? Is it physically or spiritually?"

Mrs. Miller took a moment to understand my question and then said, "Physically, of course! The angels took him up before the eyes of many of his disciples. Not only that the angels will also bring him down to earth in the same manner as they raised him up." She looked happy and radiant. I also felt happy for her, because we also believe the same about Jesus' ascent to heaven from the description of the Quran (4:156-158), and also of his second coming from a series of predictions made by Prophet Muhammad. But without mentioning any of it, I said, "Mrs. Miller, if you truly believe so, you should also believe Jesus did not die on the Cross and he was also buried alive."

"May I please know why?"

"I mean, if Jesus was raised to heaven physically, it means he certainly didn't die on the Cross and he was also buried alive. In that case, the question of Jesus' resurrection does not arise at all, because the primary or the prior condition of resurrection is death. So, resurrection from one's own death and rising from the dead, as the Gospel describes about Jesus in Luke 24:46, is not the same. Is not the graveyard a place for the dead?"

"You may think so," Mrs. Miller said with a mild objection, "But it doesn't apply to Jesus. We believe Jesus died and resurrected after three days in his own form and then he ascended to heaven physically."

"It is what you believe but Jesus' own words and acts tell us he did not die on the Cross and he was also buried alive. I already provided sufficient evidence from the Gospel in support of that. Let me narrate to you another well-known episode of Jesus' appearance to his disciples from the Gospel of Luke. I hope you will ponder over the matter seriously after I read it. You will find this description in Luke 24:39-41" I said to her while browsing on the file of my lap. After I got it, I said, "I will only read that part after Jesus rose from his grave and appeared in the room among his eleven disciples saying, *Peace be upon you*. We may now check what Jesus said or did to pacify them when they mistook him for a ghost or spirit and became terrified.

"Jesus tried to convince his frightening disciples that he was his old self, and he did not die. Showing his hands and feet, Jesus said to them,

"Look at my hands and my feet. It is I myself! Touch me and see; a ghost does not have flesh and bones, as you see I have.

When he had said this, he showed them his hands and feet. And while they still did not believe it because of joy and amazement, he asked them, "Do you have anything here to eat?" They gave him a piece of broiled fish, and he took it and ate it in their presence.

After I finished reading, I asked, "Mrs. Miller, doesn't this description match perfectly with a man who somehow escaped from his imminent death and appeared to his own people being exhausted and hungry, and also expecting their love, support and shelter for his survival and safety?"

Mrs. Miller did not answer. Looking at her impassive face, I could not help saying, "I really have no idea how Jesus' devoted followers could believe in his death or resurrection, after he has left for them such a vivid instance in his own words and deeds?"

"Yes, I understand your confusion." Mrs. Miller responded trying to maintain her patience and politeness, "But we believe in Jesus' resurrection, because Jesus proved it himself by fulfilling his own prophecy."

"May I please know about his prophecy?"

"You will find it in Matthew 12:40."

"Just give me a second." When I opened my book and found it, I felt happy and excited because I intended to end my discussion with this prophecy of Jesus. I just did not know why Mrs. Miller chose this prophecy in support of Jesus' atonement or resurrection.

Jesus' prophecy referring to Jonah nullifies the validity of his atonement and resurrection both

I tried to listen to her carefully when she began to read: *For as Jonah was three days and three nights in the belly of a huge fish, so the Son of Man will be three days and three nights in the heart of the earth.*

Mrs. Miller asked me after she read, "By the way Madam, do you know who Jonah was, and what caused him to go into the belly of the whale?"

"Yes, very well. We call him Prophet Yunus. There is also a separate chapter (10) in the Quran by his name. He is also mentioned in other places of the Quran. The reason for his going into the belly of the whale or a huge fish, is same as we find in the description of the Bible. But Jonah is especially remembered by most of the Muslims for one of his brief supplications that he made to God in the darkness of the whale's belly. He admitted of his fault in sincere repentance and said to God, *"There is no God but You, Glory be to You! Indeed, I was the one who committed wrong.* (21:87)

"You may feel amazed to know," I added further, "That Muslims all over the world still make this supplication whenever they face any kind of affliction in their life."

"I find it really amazing." Mrs. Miller said in appreciation.

Then she told me, "Since you know about Jonah so well, you will also understand why Jesus compared his resurrection with Jonah's coming out from the belly of the fish."

"May I please know how?"

"By this comparison," Mrs. Miller began to explain, "Jesus made it clear to all that he went inside his grave as Jonah went inside the belly of the fish. Then like Jonah inside the belly of the fish, he also stayed inside his grave for three days and three nights. Finally, he came out from his grave as did Jonah from the belly of the fish. I hope now you know," she asked me very confidently, "Why we believe in Jesus' atonement and in his resurrection, right?"

"I wish I could," I said to her trying to hide my frustration, "You have quoted this prophecy without even trying to know what Jesus really meant by it. Otherwise, you could see for yourself this one prophecy of Jesus would be enough to nullify the validity of his atonement and resurrection both."

"I think you are questioning my common sense." Mrs. Miller sounded a bit offended.

"I hope you'll excuse me for that after I explain to you what Jesus really meant by this prophecy. The Bible tells us a huge fish swallowed Jonah the moment the boatmen threw him into the raging sea. Then the fish carried him in its belly for three days and three nights and then threw him up on a land by the command of God. Right?"

"Right."

"Do you know the vital point you have missed in this prophecy?"

"What do you mean by the vital point?" Mrs. Miller asked me back in apprehension.

"The vital point is Jonah was alive when the fish swallowed him, he was alive inside the belly of the fish for three days and three nights, and he was also alive when the fish threw him up on the land by the command of God. Similarly, Jesus was alive after he was crucified, he was alive after he was buried, and he was also alive after he came out from his grave. I hope, now you understand why I said this one prophecy of Jesus is enough to nullify the validity of his atonement and resurrection both."

Mrs. Miller looked sad and remained silent for a while and then asked in a weak voice, "But how could Jesus live inside his grave for three days and three nights?"

"I think you should have asked first how Jonah lived in the belly of the whale which carried him deep in the oceans for three days and three nights! But keeping my question to myself, I said. Jesus was alive inside his grave for several reasons. The heavy mixture of about hundred-pound weight (John 19: 29) that Jesus' two disciples put all over his body helped him to heal his wounds and to regain his consciousness. Then the newly dug tomb where Jesus was buried, was known to be spacious and because of that the air inside the tomb was good enough to make him breathe easily. Besides that, the Angels of God also made it easy and safe for him by removing the heavy stone from the entrance of his tomb (Matthew 28:2), and guarding him against all kinds of harm or mischief until he came out from his grave safely. Not only that," I said to her last reminding, "The Gospel also tells us Jesus stayed in his tomb only for two nights and one day." (Mark 15:42-47; 16: 2-6)

Mrs. Miller was indeed a good listener. She looked at her wristwatch after I stopped and then picked up her water-bottle from the side table and began to sip unmindfully.

Jesus' followers chose to play the role of 'Doubting-Thomas'

I also looked at the digital wall-clock in front of me. It was five ten. It means we still had fifty minutes before she leaves. I felt happy because it was the first time, I completed my talk on Jesus' atonement with someone who was a devout Christian and at the same time learned and highly educated. Despite of that, I felt deeply concerned for her, because looking at her impassive face and distant look in her eyes, I thought like many of my ordinary missionary friends, she also chose to play the role of 'Doubting-Thomas.' To understand the meaning and implication of this reference, I need to describe in brief who is Thomas, and why I have mentioned him as Doubting-Thomas.

The Gospel tells us Thomas was one of the disciples of Jesus. He was absent when Jesus appeared to his other disciples after he came out from his grave. But Thomas did not believe them at all when they told him later about Jesus' visit and what he did or said to them. Not only that, Thomas doubted them so much that he said to them straight, *"Unless I see the nail-marks in his hands and put my fingers where the nails were, and put my hands into his sides, I will not believe."* (John 20:24-25)

Thomas' doubt in the words of his own close and reliable friends, made me think that my learned guest Mrs. Miller also had the same problem to take my words seriously though I tried to say everything from the Gospel- the Book she believes herself as a true account of Jesus' own words and deeds. So, to utilize my last few minutes, I asked her, "By the way Mrs. Miller, do you remember what Thomas did when his close friends described to him about Jesus' reappearance to them after he rose from his grave?"

"Yes, he refused to believe them." Mrs. Miller answered in brief while putting down her empty water-bottle inside her handbag.

"Do you think he had any particular reason to doubt his close friends?"

"No."

"But he did, right?"

"Yes."

"Similarly," I said to her lightly, "You also have no reason to doubt what I narrated to you from the Gospel about Jesus and what he asked his people to do for the remission of their sin and for their eternal life in heaven, but you did, right?"

In her silence, I continued, "I think you also remember that Thomas was very lucky because he believed the words of his friends completely when Jesus reappeared to them only after eight days. Right?" (John 20:26–29)

"Right."

"Do you think Mrs. Miller," I asked her kidding but meaning seriously, "You can afford to wait until Jesus arrives at the end of the world and reminds you that he did not die on the Cross for your sin or for your eternal life in heaven?"

Mrs. Miller ignored my question and asked me instead excitedly, "Do you believe in Jesus' Second Coming?"

"Yes, undoubtedly. The Quran has mentioned of his second coming as one of the major signs of the Last Hour meaning the end of the world. (43:61) Besides that, Muhammad-the last Prophet of God has also left for us a vivid description on Jesus' second coming in a series of his predictions."

"May I please know what he has said?" She asked me very sweetly.

Looking at the radiant glow on her beautiful face I said, "He has mentioned clearly where Jesus would descend from heaven and how he would look at that moment."

"O my God! May I please know what else he said?"

"He also said that Jesus would fight with the antichrist and other enemies of God and he would defeat them all. Then he would rule the world following the commands of God to maintain peace, progress, and justice for all of mankind. In other word, Jesus will finally establish on earth the promised kingdom of God that you've been preaching now from door to door."

"Do you have those books with you? Can I please borrow them?" Mrs. Miller asked me, pleading.

"But Mrs. Miller," I asked her back trying to be nice and polite, "Why do you want to know what Jesus might say or do at that time when your skulls and bones might turn into dust? Is not it much better to utilize your time, energy and intelligence to learn and follow what Jesus already taught you by the command of God when you are still young and alive?"

My question fused all the radiance and glow from her face in a moment, and it made me feel so bad that I asked her at once, "Please forgive me Mrs. Millar. I have no right to advise you like that."

"It is okay, Madam. I should rather thank you for your reminder."

"Thanks a lot for your being so nice and patient to me. I just wanted you to know we should not take our faith blindly. If we think of our faith seriously, we will find it is like riding a bus without knowing where it will go but believing it would take us to our destination. Similarly, we have been following the faith of our parents without knowing whether they are right or wrong, but believing it is right. Just think for a moment what might happen to your unquestioning faith in Jesus' dying for your sin if you were born and brought up in a Muslim family like me! Similarly, I would believe in that without a question if I were born and brought up like you in a Christian family. Right?"

Mrs. Miller did not answer.

I tried to ignore her silence and asked, "Do you think, God's guidance for mankind will turn to be right or wrong according to the change of their birth, parents, or ethnicity? Or it should always remain the same or unchanged regardless to their time, place, race or religion?"

In her silence, I asked her again, "Don't you think all of us should be in the same boat if we believe undoubtedly God is our ultimate Refuge and we have to go back to Him one day from this transitory station of our life? It is the only reason, our faith in God and in His guidance should be prudent and reflective instead of being blind or self-made. At the same time we should also remember our life on this earth is short and uncertain, and we have no chance to correct our mistake once we cross the one way exit of death and find us there in a wrong place."

A few heavy moments passed after I stopped.

"Madam, will you mind if I leave now?" Mrs. Miller broke her silence and asked sweetly.

"Sure. I hope you will not be late to attend your party, right?"

"Don't worry, it is not yet five-thirty. But thanks a lot for sharing your thoughts and knowledge with me. It has really been a fruitful discussion for me." Mrs. Miller said in appreciation while putting her Bible carefully inside her handbag.

"It is actually you my dear young friend," I admitted to her truthfully, "Who deserves the thanks, because it is for your endless patience and tolerance, I could talk to you so freely about this most delicate topic of your faith."

"By the way Madam," she asked me before she walked to the door, "May I please have your telephone number?"

"Sure." I jotted down my telephone number on a piece of paper and gave it to her.

"Thanks."

"You are most welcome."

When I opened the door for her, she asked me again startling, "Madam, would you mind, if I come again soon with some of my seniors?"

"Of course not," I said enthusiastically. "I think that would be great and wonderful."

"Thanks. I will call you before I come," She said smiling. "Until then stay happy and safe."

Reverend,

That was nine years ago since I completed writing this book and another eleven years have passed after I edited my published book for the third time, and I am still waiting for her call.

No compulsion in religion! Truth stands clear from error, and he who rejects false deities and believes in God, has grasped a firm handhold that never breaks. And God hears and knows all things.

God is the Protecting Friend of those who have faith. From the depth of darkness, He will bring them into light. ......
(Quran 2:256-257)

Afterword

An Unexpected Disruption

Reverend,

One morning, about a week or so after my last conversation with Mrs. Miller, when I was busy editing my last letter to you, I had a phone call from my old friend Ruby, who had settled in Houston long before I came to America. I felt her voice choked with a kind of strange and unexplained emotion as she asked, "Are you watching TV?"

"No. Why?"

"Turn it on and watch."

"Which channel?" I asked

"Any channel," she said, and then hung up her telephone, putting me in a pool of worries and anxieties.

After I turned my TV on, I felt myself pinned to the ground as I watched in the CNN a replay of what had happened a few moments ago. First, I thought it was an unfortunate accident as I watched a plane crash into the Hightower in the New York City, followed by another plane almost simultaneously. But when I understood my mistake, I only wished I never saw or heard any of it. My heart completely broke as if, by a sudden blow of shock, shame, and utter disbelief, when I came to know gradually that it was a horrendous suicidal attack, launched by a group of zealots, claiming proudly they did it for the sake of Allah and for His religion-Islam. Their foolish act followed by their false claim made me feel so ashamed, low, and humiliated that I wished nobody knew here I was a Muslim. I think Muslims all over the world felt the same as I did at that moment.

Reverend, in that situation, the Western Media began to add fuel to the fire by playing a vindictive role against Islam, with the help of the well- reputed evangelists like you and others. They seemed to compete each other to prove who could denounce Islam the most through their frequent appearance in the public TV. If some of them blamed Islam as a religion of evil, others claimed its adherents being arrogant, hostile, and fond of killing or taking revenge. If someone called Muhammad-the Prophet of Islam a terrorist, the next one denounced the Quran as a book teaching violence and hatred among his followers. Some of them even ridiculed the name of Allah, whom the Muslims call or invoke in Arabic in place of His English name God. They found the God of the Christians bigger and more real than the God of the Muslims. Others said the God of the Muslims asked them to sacrifice their lives for Him to go to heaven, while the God of the Christians sacrificed His only Son to purify them and to take them to heaven!

Thus they continued this nonstop anti-Islamic propaganda against a religion of nearly one-fifth population of the world, because a fraction of the fractions of its misled adherents did some cruelest and most foolish act in the name of their religion. While listening to those accusations from so many scholars and religious gurus of the Western world, I could hardly expect Mrs. Miller to visit me again or ever. Neither did I expect any devoted follower of Jesus Christ to read my book which I wrote in reply to your self-made comment about the God of Islam being different from the Christians or the God of the Judeo-Christian faith. So, I abandoned my most cherished dream to publish my book and to present it to the audience of the Western world to help them verify the truth of your comment about the God of Islam being different from the God of the Judeo-Christian faith.

As the days passed into months and the months into years, I noticed the national TV channels eventually got tired of playing a one-sided game on attacking against Islam. They started inviting some Muslim scholars to talk about various sides of Islam. Then I felt amazed to notice that curiosity toward Islam seemed to grow in people's mind slowly but steadily. Some of them started reading books on Islam written by the open-minded scholars of the Western world. Even some of them began to read the meaning of the Quran, life of Muhammad and even started learning the language and the culture of the Arabs.

Reverend, a few years after the horrendous attack of 9/11, while watching CNN I saw you in the inset of the TV screen to take questions from John King, one of its chief correspondents. He asked you to know about your reflection on your comments that you made before about Islam being a very evil and wicked religion and the God of Islam being different from the God of the Jews and the Christians. I waited eagerly for your answer. You looked a little hesitant at first. As far as I remember, you did not answer the first part of his question. But in reply to the second part, you said the God of the Christians had a Son whom He sent to sacrifice for their sin, but the god of Islam had no son and He sent none to redeem their sin.

Another day, I saw you taking questions from Paula Zahn, the young and beautiful news staff of CNN. In reply to her question about your reflection on Islam, you responded promptly that it was a complicated religion. Then she asked you sweetly whether you had ever studied Islam to which you admitted honestly that you did not. But Paula was too good to ask you back how did you find Islam was a complicated religion without knowing anything about it?

Reverend, I owe my sincere thanks to you to help my dream come true, because it is your interesting observation about Islam and the God of Islam that steered me up once again to look at my manuscript in the forgotten file of my lap and to publish it finally for the people of the Western world. In recognition to that great help, I sincerely wish you, your family, friends and devoted followers a long meaningful life with full of spirit and strength, health and happiness and above all, with patience and perseverance to seek for the truth, following the advice of Jesus where he said:

If you hold to my teaching, you are really my disciples. Then you will know the truth, and the truth will set you free. (John 8:31-32)

Bibliography

1. King James Versions (KJV), Thomas Nelson Publishers, Nashville, 1977

2. New Revised Standard Versions (NRSV), The Harper Collins Study Bible, Harper, San Francisco

3. The New International Versions (NIV), New World Translations of the Bible,

4. The Dictionary of the Bible, By John Mckenzie,

5. The Holy Quran with Arabic Text, & English Translation, By Muhammad M. Pickthal, Kutubkhana Ishayat-ul-Islam, Delhi, India

6. The Holy Quran Text, Translation and Commentary, By A. Yusuf Ali, Amana Corp, Brentwood, Maryland 20722, 1983

7. Interpretation of the Meanings of the Noble Quran in English, By Dr. Muhammad Taqi-ud-Din Al-Hilali And Dr. Muhammad Muhsin Khan, Maktaba Dar-us-Salam, Riyadh 11475, Saudi Arabia, 1993

8. English Translation of the meaning of Al-Quran, By Muhammad Farooq-i-Azam Malik, The Institute of Islamic Knowledge, Houston, Texas, 1998

9. Merriam-Webster's Encyclopedia of World Religions, Springfield, MA 01102, 1999.

10. The Concise Encyclopedia of Islam, By Cyril Glasse, Harper Collins, New York, NY 10022

11. Muhammad in the Veda and the Puranas, Translated in English by Muhammad Alamgir, from its Bengali Version by Prof. Ashitkumar Bandopaddhaya; from its original Hindi transcript by Dr. Ved Prakash Upapaddhaya, a great

research scholar of Sanskrit Prayag University in India.

12. What Is His Name? By Ahmed Deedat, IPCI, Durban 4000, RSA, 1997.

13. Al-Quran-the Miracles of Miracles, By Ahmed Deedat, IPCI, Durban 4001, South Africa

14. Muhammad (pbuh) the Greatest, By Ahmed Deedat, IPCI, Durban 4001, South Africa

15. The Choice: Islam and Christianity, By Ahmed Deedat, IPCI, Durban 4001, South Africa

16. Jesus a Prophet of Islam, By Muhammad Ataur Rahim, Millat Book Center, Delhi 110053, India

17. What did Jesus really say? By Misha'l Ibn Abdullah, Islamic Assembly of North America, Ann Arbor, MI 48105, 1996.

18. The Bible's Last Prophet By Faisal Siddiqui Al Saadawi Publications Alexandria VA 22303, 1995

19. Muhammad: His life based on the earlier sources, by Martin Lings, George Allen & Unwin, UK, 1983.

20. The Vision of Islam, by Sachico Murata and William C. Chittic, Lahore, Pakistan, 1998.

21. Trialogue of The Abrahamic Faith, By Ismail Raji, Amana Publications, Beltsville, MD 20705, 1995

22. Is Jesus God? The Bible Says No, By Shabir Ally, Al-Attique International Islamic Publications, Toronto, Canada, 1998

23. Follow Jesus or Follow Paul, By Dr. Roshan Enam, Al-Attique International Islamic Publications, Toronto, Canada, 1997

24. The Bible led me to Islam, By Abdul-Malik Leblank, Dar

Al Hadyan, Riyadh, Saudi Arabia, 1997

25. What Christians and Muslims should know about themselves By Robert W. Mond, The Forum For Islamic Work, Flushing, New York, 11355

26. The Dead Sea Scrolls, The Gospel of Barnabas, and The New Testament, By M.A Yusseff, American Trust Publications, Indianapolis, Indiana 46231, 1994

27. What the Bible Says About Muhammad (pbuh), By Ahmed Deedat, IPCI, Durban 4001, South Africa, 1998

28. Crucifixion or Cruci-Fiction, By Ahmed Deedat, IPCI, Durban 4001, SA, 1998

29. The Life and Work of Muhammad, By Yahiya Emerick, Alpha Books, Indianapolis, IN 46240

30. Jesus will Return, By Harun Yahya, Ta-Ha Publications, London, SW9, OBB, 2006

31. Izhar-Ul-Haq (Truth Revealed) part 1-4, By Maulana M.Rahamatullah Kairanvi, Ta-Ha Publishers, London, Sw9 OBB, UK, 1992

32. Riyad-us-Saliheen, Vol Two, (# 1808) By Al-Imam Abu Zakariya Yahya bin Sharif An-Nawawi Ad-Dimashqi, translated by Dr. Muhammad Amin Abu Usamah Al Arabi bin Razduk, Darussalam, Riyadh 11416, Saudi Arabia, 1999

33. Zakir Naik's Lectures in Peace TV

Feedback from the distinguished readers

One God for All by D. R. BANU

Reading Ms Banu's manuscript, I was reminded of a conversation I had about 30 year ago when a dear friend of mine asked if I believed in God. At that time I was still an Evangelical Christian (at least on paper) living in Switzerland. I have since converted to Islam and live in the US.

My answer was and I can remember time, setting and circumstances as if it just happened yesterday: "Yes I believe in God but I have a hard time believing in Jesus as God's son and the entire Trinity approach."

Looking back obviously makes one see much clearer and it proves that God's guidance set me off in the right direction many years before of my becoming a Muslim. It is indeed the concept of "tawhid", believing in the One and only God, which like no other fundament of our joint belief system as the three monotheistic religions, is at the heart of our salvation. The mere fact that we do talk about monotheism as the binding link between all of us suggests, God is One and only One.

I believe this book to focus on the most essential issue that guides us as believers in God. I am not very familiar with the Bible so this book allows Muslims valuable insights in its teachings and therefore a broader horizon to discuss issues of "tawhid" in an informed dialogue with Christian colleagues and friends. On the other hand it invites Christians to get a good overview of the Quran's teachings touching the most important common issue of our joint faith without reading the entire Book which of course is very much recommended nonetheless.

The book by Dil Banu as she herself suggests, is not one more scholarly attempt to clarify the commonalities and differences most notably between the Christian and Islamic practice of "tawhid" but chooses a very unique and refreshing approach by ways of a dozen letters addressed to the well-known Reverend Franklin Graham in response to his assertions that we do not worship the same God. Furthermore, it lives of its dialogues between the Author and various missionaries who often visit her to make their case for Trinity and Jesus as the only way for salvation.

Many books, as the author admits herself, have been written on the topic. However, the unique approach to writing this book and the strong focus on the essential arguments for a truly monotheistic "tawhid" as prescribed by God in the Quran and the Bible, make "One God for All" a book that I can recommend very highly to Christians and Muslims alike to read.

Allow me to just quote one sign (ayah) of the Quran here in conclusion: Ibrahim (14:52): "Here is a message for mankind. Let them take warning therefrom. And let them know that HE Is (no other than) One God: Let men of understanding take heed."

Blessed are those who treasure this truth in their souls.

Eduard Tschan, PhD., Senior Adviser Community Health Workers, at American Red Cross previously Country Director in Haiti for the International Red Cross.

In our times of strife and alienation, the author presents a fresh argument for harmony and togetherness. She has a deep understanding of the human mind through ages in which God eternally leaves His unifying marks. God's Omnipresence binds our ageless humanity on one hand, and on the other, it directs us to His singular message of Unity. The author essentially focuses on the Unity of God and articulates its dimensions from the vantage point of her Islamic conviction. In so doing, she places other religions vis-à-vis Islam and vice versa. In keeping with the spirit of Islam, she never indulges in the denigration of the other. She does encounter anti- Islamism that we see in vogue. Her style is unapologetic and straight to the point. She takes the antagonists to the task. But her tone, all throughout, is one of first reconciliation. She seeks to make her audience understand her belief-system, i. e. Islam, and in turn, understand the misunderstanding of Islam by her audience. Her audience, obviously, is Western (if not exclusively), and as such, her arguments flourish in the Western context. She does leave room for the watchful non-Western Muslim and non-Muslim readers to get hold of that context. The book addressing timeless issues is quintessentially timely.

Muhammad Mashreque was a professor of English at Allen University, Columbia, SC. Besides, he works with such organizations as uniting adherents of the Faith (i.e. CAIR) and promoting ethnic- racial harmony.

"One God for All" is an interesting and contemplative work, delving deep into the ancient texts of both the Bible and the Quran, to uncover the ties which bind Christianity and Islam to each other, and the origins from which differing practices and beliefs have stemmed. People of all religious backgrounds can benefit from this thorough and informative text. "One God for All" surprises us with its hidden gems of knowledge, sure to intrigue and enlighten even the most learned of readers.

Christina Keating Sami, Maryland

Though Dil. R. Banu's letters are addressed specially to Reverend Sir Franklin Graham, it will surely capture a wide audience to engage in the same conversation with her. Her dire need to clarify the rather widely debated topic; do the Muslims, Jews and the Christians worship the same God? will unravel the misconceptions laid out in the Religious world of today. This question was probably the catalyst that started her conversations with Reverend Sir Franklin Graham.

With current technologies and overload of information, Dil Banu's letters are simple and yet meticulously detailed to give the reader the understanding of the fundamental beliefs of the Muslims who share the same Abrahamic faith with both the Jews and the Christians.

Her collection of letters are well organized and easy to read. She also provides good resources from both the Quranic and the Biblical texts which confirms her beliefs and statements. These texts will also guide the readers to pay attention to factual details.

"Remember this everlasting covenant of God which He meant to be obeyed and observed by Abraham and by all his progeny" (Letter-3), is the cornerstone of her letter which becomes the connecting factor that will unite those who share the same Abrahamic faith.

Though religious toleration is highly encouraged in her letters, the author is certainly unapologetic in stating her firm belief in worshiping the same One God of the Judeo-Christian Faith.

Merriam-Webster Encyclopedia of World Religions (page 747) defines: Islamic monotheism is more literal and uncompromising than that of any other religion. Allah is confessed being one, eternal, unbegotten, unequaled and beyond partnership of any kind.

A well-researched and comparative reading, written passionately.

Diyana Abdullah, Richmond, VA

We are teachers by profession and our two sons have completed their 10th Grade. From our long experience as both parents and teachers, we strongly feel that this book "One God For All," is a must read book for the young generations of all religions especially for the Christians and the Muslims who have now a days, lots of reservations against one another for some obvious and unavoidable reasons. We believe this book will certainly help them to identify the root or the heritage of their own faith and to look at each other with love, respect, and trust.

We like to thank and appreciate the author and the Publisher very much for giving us a chance to read such an enlightening, spiritual and thought-provoking book as this. We also look forward to see her next book in reply to the evangelist's comment against Islam.

Md. Ziaul Haque Chowdhury & Towhida Yesmin Chowdhury, Maryland

---

About Reverend Franklin Graham

William Franklin Graham, known to all as Reverend Franklin Graham, is an American Christian evangelist and a dedicated missionary. He was born in July 14, 1952 in Asheville, North Carolina and his father is a well reputed and much respected evangelist Billy Graham.

Rev. Franklin Graham had his education in the Stony Brook School, Appalachian State University and Le Tourneau University. He married Jane Austin Cunningham in 1974 and had four children through this marriage.

Rev. Graham is the founder of Samaritan's Purse-a world relief fund for the poor and needy. He is also the president and CEO of Billy Graham Evangelist Association. He has become an international Christian for his relief and missionary work throughout the world.

Despite of his busy missionary life, he also wrote some books especially for the children. Some of them are: Kids praying For Kids, Operation Christmas Child, and Miracles in a shoebox.

Rev. Franklin Graham has made himself a controversial religious personality through many of his abrupt, unauthentic, and demeaning comments against Islam-the latest and the fastest growing religion of nearly one-fourth population of the world today.

About The Author

Dil. R. Banu, a Muslim by birth and practice, a retired lecturer from a prestigious school of her homeland Bangladesh, settled in America about thirty years ago. She worked as a substitute teacher in the local elementary schools for a year or so and then she began to operate a licensed family daycare in her rented apartment where all her neighbors were Christians. This job was a turning point in her life. It made her a writer from a daycare provider.

Her favorite subject is Comparative Religion since her teenage. She loves to know about God and His religions that people of the world believe and follow in His name. She finds it amazing when people follow different religions in the name of the same God but claim equally except them all are misled and are destined for eternal hell.

She thinks man's faith in God should be prudent and reflective instead of being blind or self-made. As their life on this earth is short and most uncertain, and they have no chance to correct their mistakes once they cross the one way exit of death and find them in a wrong place, she believes the sooner they identify the true path of God and try to follow it, the better for them.

About The Book

Utilizing the Holy Scriptures-the Bible and the Quran both, this book "One God For All" presents a series of letters written to the well-known American evangelist Franklin Graham in reply to the first part of his comment where he said, "The god of Islam is not the same God of the Christian or the Judeo-Christian faith. It is a different god." Then he said, "And I believe Islam is a very evil and a very wicked religion."

The author who is a Muslim by birth and practice, found his comment not only unauthentic but malicious and misleading for the people of the Western world-especially the Christians who hardly know anything about the God of the Muslims or their religion Islam.

Based on the countless evidence from both parts of the Bible and the Quran-the last and the final guidebook of God, the author has made it distinctly clear that the Muslims comprising now about one-fourth population of the world, have still been worshiping the same One God of Jesus, Moses, and Abraham since Muhammad was sent last reviving, rectifying, and restoring their pure monotheistic faith in Islam, about fourteen hundred years ago.

Pacific Book Review About
Author's Second Book
Anna Asked Was Muhammad A Prophet?
[Her question is answered from the Bible and other major scriptures of the world]
By Aaron Washington

Author Dil R. Banu first started by defining what prophecy is. I was impressed with her detailed explanation as it made me have a deeper understanding of the definition and why God's people are referred to as prophets. There are so many people who claim to be prophets in today's world. This can be confusing to believers who follow anyone who proclaims the word. The author further expounded on the subject of false prophecy with a Bible verse (Duet 18:21-22). Through that verse, we learn the true prophets make correct prophesies, but it is God who inspires them. False prophets, on the other hand, rely on their imagination, making them fail most of the times.

Dil R. Banu's intent when writing Anna Asked Was Muhammad a Prophet was to show the link between Muhammad and the prophets in the Bible. Christianity and Islam may operate on a different basis, but the fact remains that there are some fundamental beliefs in both the Quran and the Bible which link the two. This is what the author wants everyone to understand. Anna Asked Was Muhammad a Prophet, is a religious book which helps even the unobservant and least interested readers know more about religion and Prophet Muhammad. It is amazing how the author broke everything down. I learned much about Islam teachings vis-a-vis the Christian gospel by the end of my read.

One of the most fascinating parts in the book was when the author explained the relation between Muhammad, Jesus, and Moses. Contrary to popular belief, Muhammad was not like Jesus. He was more like Moses. This is because Jesus was born of the Virgin Mary, in a miraculous way. Both Moses and Muhammad, however, were born to a married couple. The two later got married and had their own offspring. The next comparison between Moses and Muhammad versus Jesus was that the two were accepted, obeyed, and respected by most of their people as the true messengers of God in their own lifetime. This was not the case with Jesus. Jews rejected Jesus and his mission and even claimed that he was not the true Messiah. Dil R. Banu's discussion of the three brought about a lot of clarity to this history. At the end of the day, I was able to tell the three apart and noted the roles they played.

Reading Anna Asked Was Muhammad a Prophet, gave me the impression of going through the Bible and the Quran simultaneously. The author did a fantastic job by writing this book as it helped me have a better understanding of the two books. Dil R. Banu's book is nothing short of informative. The author is engaging too and wrote from an informed point of view. Other than her way of explaining things, I have to mention the author's choice of words was another thing that made this book easy to read. The language used is simple with the exception of a few technical words which are well outlined in the text. This book is ideal for a wide range of reading audiences from early adult on up, and of virtually any faith, with any degree of religious background.

Just Published!
AUTHOR'S NEXT BOOK
ABRAHAM WAS COMMANDED TO SACRIFICE
ISHMAEL-HIS FIRSTBORN

[Based on the Bible, Quran, and other reliable sources]

www.ingramcontent.com/pod-product-compliance
Lightning Source LLC
Chambersburg PA
CBHW071442070526
44578CB00001B/201